ROGER DRUITT was sui
growing up on a farm. Sii
wanted to understand the ˄
meet Anthroposophy in his teens. He studied mathematics at Cambridge, graduating in Economics to work in
computing. He discovered the Anthroposophical Society and the
Christian Community in the 1960s and has enjoyed the inspiration of
both movements ever since, teaching widely on aspects of Nature
observation and connecting to the hidden spirit. He is the author of
Festivals of the Year, A Workbook for Re-enlivening the Christian Festive Cycle.
Roger lives in Sussex and has four adult children, many grandchildren and
thousands of bees. He enjoys travelling to teach the work of *this* book.

OBSERVING NATURE'S SECRET

Practical Exercises for Perceiving Soul and Spirit

Roger Druitt

PS 11   ex 1
PS 13   ex 2
   16   ex 3

RUDOLF STEINER PRESS

Rudolf Steiner Press
Hillside House, The Square
Forest Row, East Sussex RH18 5ES

www.rudolfsteinerpress.com

Published by Rudolf Steiner Press 2018

A catalogue record for this book is available from the British Library

ISBN 978 1 85584 546 6

Cover by Andrew Morgan Design incorporating a photo, 'Nature observes her Secret', by
Roger Druitt
Typeset by DP Photosetting, Neath, West Glamorgan
Printed and bound by 4Edge Ltd., Essex

CONTENTS

My grateful thanks go to all who helped me bring this work to expression:

Anastasia, Anne, Francis, Gill, Heidi, Helen, Hugh, Jane, Louis, Peter, Sophy, Sue and Thomas; and additional special thanks to Heidi Herrmann for helping make it happen and Sevak Gulbekian for the title.

Also to Ann, with whom much of the research was shared.

PREFACE

At the age of three, I demanded of my mother that she explain the whole world to me. Twelve years later, she began to attend an Anthroposophical study group on Rudolf Steiner's cosmology. He was a thinker and spiritual researcher of the nineteenth and twentieth centuries who gave insights of understanding for all spheres of life. She learned there that it was not helpful to talk about the content to under-21s but I interrogated her each week nonetheless, gleaning quite a few valuable fragments of Steiner's teaching methods and revelations. I was already accustomed to silently rejecting some of the things presented at school as fact but stored them all up anyway. In contrast, these weekly fragments were marked for me with the stamp of truth. That was and still is my method of study: letting everything seen and thought live on in the mind till it sorts itself out. That turns out to be the method recommended by Steiner for a secure development of knowledge, combined with an artistic judgement. One of the results is this book. It contains many citations from Rudolf Steiner. They are not meant to prove anything but are given only so the reader can access the written source if inclined to do so. What I have written is upon my own authority, either from observation or from a full grasp and interweaving of the relevant ideas. Thus my mother fulfilled my demand through connecting me to this source of investigation, for which I am grateful. Anthroposophy has been a good research tool for me ever since and has been useful and fruitful in every sphere of my life.

At four, I was allowed to wander wherever I wanted in the 'large' wood next to our house. I became sensitive to the different trees and shrubs that grew there and the flowers of the different seasons. There were certain plants and certain types of ground I did not want to go near, for example those with a certain odour, or where it was dark, damp or thorny. Other areas gave an atmosphere of goodness and nurturing. All this I took for granted as being what the world was like: something that surrounded you and spoke to you through its moods and gestures. On moving into a town at around ten, I still felt that the most important activity that one could carry out in spare time was gathering flowers in those wilder areas just outside civilization. This activity seemed to express the relationship to nature where there is both giving and receiving: one gives one's soul back to the world through the enjoyment of the flowers one has picked. This is an activity that I still regard as important work for the future of Nature.

Years later, I sat in a classroom, part of my priest training, when in came a man to teach us about plants. He was of few words but spoke with his presence. This was a paradisal time for us who attended because week by week we had courses from people from all over the world who were world leaders in their subject. So too was this man. He held up plants to awaken our eye to their contrast; and because of his inner stillness and a long life of observing plants, his own feeling for them seemed to quicken our power of observation. My wife-to-be, Ann, participated in the course too and we were mightily inspired and transformed by the theme and its messenger and went on being transformed by their fruits for the rest of our lives.

Eighteen months later I saw his name on a book spine in the library of the priest holding my final interview before ordination in 1970 and not many days after that I discovered that he had died around that time. This man was Frits Julius. His books are available in Dutch and German and some also in English. I recommend his article on a journey with elemental beings (*The Golden Blade*, 1971) which helps one become more at home with the realm behind the sense world.

Half a century has elapsed since then so in his memory I am writing down and dedicating to him, as one of my spiritual teachers throughout these subsequent years, the fruits of the work that he set in motion in my life, inspired by the powerful memory-picture of him sweeping his arm in the curve of the great Mars Loops in the sky as the archetype of the curving branch of a shrub.

I do not call my work Goethean Observation because this expression is often used without the relevant awareness of what Goethe had to say on the subject and is often no more than phenomenology. J.W. von Goethe was a thoroughgoing observer who brought a powerful thinking into his observing and guided this thinking in an artistic way. He observed and wrote in great depth on many things besides plants; but with plants he unfolded the concept of the '*Urpflanze*' or 'archetypal plant' as it is referred to in English. This is something *seen with the thinking*, so 'Goetheanism' is really much more than mere observation. It is something in the realm of thinking that arises through making a *connection to Goethe through his ideas*. Goethe developed picture-thoughts through his scientific research and expressed them in poetic or epithet forms. By living into one of these one can find that the thought becomes alive and can grow further within one's own mind. Rudolf Steiner links this phenomenon to the fact that the

Resurrection (of Christ) is not just an event but a *process* that continues into the future and in which thoughts that are already alive can go on developing in this way. (*Die geistigen Hintergründe des Ersten Weltkrieges*, GA 174b, lecture of 26.04.18, apparently not translated into English.) The mind is discovered as a place where the Resurrection is revealed through this growth of spiritual seed-thoughts, although no-one would have considered ascribing it to that had not Rudolf Steiner done so. Indeed, it is just here upon the stage of thinking that the Resurrection can be *renewed*. I have attempted in this book to give examples of this (see Chapters 7 and 8).

It seems obvious that what Steiner described of this further evolving of a thought in the context of Goethe must well apply to himself too, so that his work on plant observation can develop further in the minds of his students—which would make him too a spirit guide of a new kind. I realise that Julius' approach also grew out of that source.

My work is founded on Steiner's indications, fructified here and there with Goethe's insights, which I only met later; so I consider it 'anthroposophical phenomenology'—although a somewhat heavier expression and perhaps a little pedantic, it is more accurate. One passage from one of his books, *Knowledge of Higher Worlds, How is it Attained?* has been an invaluable guideline through the years:

> It should be emphasised that the student must not lose himself in speculation on the meaning of one thing or another. Such intellectualising will only lead him away from the right road. He should look at the world with keen, healthy senses and quickened power of observation, and then give himself up to the feeling that arises within him. He should not try to make out through intellectual speculation what things mean but rather allow the things themselves to tell him. It should be remarked that artistic feeling, coupled with a quiet introspective nature, forms the best preliminary condition for the development of spiritual faculties. This feeling penetrates the superficial aspect of things and in so doing touches their secrets.

That is why this book has been worthwhile writing.

INTRODUCTION

How can you work from ordinary sense perception to a sense for the life forces that shape leaves and for the spiritual forces that create blossoms and seeds?

It helps to begin by stripping away all preconception of plant life and form. This helps one off to a fresh start. It will be easier to work with plants whose names one does not know and temporarily forget any botany one has learned until its detail becomes valuable later on. Grasping immediately at botanical identification can easily hinder the process of deeper experiencing. For example, in one round of leaf observation, participants were invited to describe a single feature they noticed. This is usually very revealing; yet one person said instead, 'It is a rhododendron leaf.' Only, it was *not* a rhododendron, so not only did we never discover what the person *had* seen but could have been misled as well. Out of this, I developed the impulse to engage people in the question, 'What can you see?' and now apply it to *Observing Nature's Secret*.

After looking at what observation can reveal, the reader will be led to observe leaves in a simple but detailed way. This gives rise to a basic grasp of features that are common to many leaves, yet vary considerably from one leaf to another. This variation is at first between different *species* of leaf, although at this stage one might not 'know' that. We have to discover it through observing and comparing; for there is also variation of shape *within* each species, to be found in the chapter on Metamorphosis. Gradually, a concept of 'leaf' is composed from the many forms, some of which are by nature arranged in sequence by the plant itself. Other steps follow, to be described in due time, after this groundwork has been established.

At the end of the book, some chapters demonstrate how the method can be applied in other fields of nature observation, opening the way for using it in all areas of life. In each case it will be shown how to access the 'individuality' manifested in what is observed: bees, rocks, colour and stars. The one on rocks touches the tricky theme of the age of the Earth. We arrive at the threshold between Matter and Spirit. Here, the 4½ billion years arrived at scientifically on the basis of radioactive decay encounters that of measuring the age by the path of the Sun through the zodiac used by Rudolf Steiner: some hundreds of thousands of years. We develop in each case a higher view that bridges over these anomalies in other areas of knowledge.

This is the scene for the work that follows. For the final stimulus to write, I thank Peter Stewart, who made it clear to me why I should do so. I also acknowledge the debt owed to the 25 years' of priest seminary students who trod the path with me and pointed out the things I had not noticed, as does Nature when one has the wit to ask questions.

1

LOOKING AT FLOWERS

The greater picture

There are many people who talk to their plants yet do not mind if you think them batty because, with a sense other than intellect, they know that the plant makes a positive response, hinted at in the line from *Four Quartets* (T.S. Eliot, 'Burnt Norton'), '*for the roses had the look of flowers that are looked at*'.

Eliot feels then that not only do plants change under the human eye and heart but that to the right eye and heart this is perceptible also by a subsequent viewer.

Let us take it for granted that for most branches of science this is all just fantasy; but let us also take it for granted that trained artists and craftsmen work out of an 'artistic science' of their training, something that *transcends* hard science rather than being 'unscientific'. Many non-artists, since they may not have gone through this training, do not know or grasp what is here being described. Others know it because they have gone through the pain of their training to enter that world; and they sense it in each other. Others still, of course, have something of this ability naturally. I hope that those who try the exercises in this book will come to share this world, where mind and heart work as it were inside one another, the mind giving sense to the heart and the heart bringing life to what has been thought—or seen.

Out of that, let us work at looking at plants.

What is a plant? It is something whose outer form is totally different from the natural forms that would arise from the chemical substances of its makeup. Carbon (and other) compounds *build* the plant but do not shape it. As minerals on their own they would make recognized geometrical forms. One can burn plants, wash the ash, then evaporate the sieved 'lye'—and crystals will form. So the plant is made of minerals but has formed itself into shapes that are not mineral but have developed through *space* (the different plant organs) *and* through time (the metamorphosis through the year that culminates with reproduction). This the mineral does not do. What makes the plant plant is something unseen, invisible to the senses. It is something, however, that we apprehend when we follow, *through* the senses, metamorphosis and gesture. Then our soul engages with the plant process as it were from within, because, rightly perceived, the changes in the plant are registered and fulfilled *within the soul*, somewhere near the heart and lungs. The 'thing' thus perceived is therefore 'supersensible', and hence an entity of a higher world: a 'being', because it '*is*', but only an *elementary* one because it has just come into existence through our own activity. Its 'isness' is not as permanent as ours is, if this can be accepted as a provisional idea; and it has its abode solely in our own soul.

This process penetrates more deeply into plant nature than the usual approach that assesses the plant for its capacity to please or for its suitability for some earthly purpose but which does not require us to go as far as the exercises of this book will take us. They will unite us with the realm of *life* that makes the plant *live*, brings us into contact with that little piece of the world of life connected to that particular plant. And this 'piece' is a being too, in the above sense, but now one not made by *our* mind but by the mind of the world. It is still 'elementary' but one degree less so than our creation; it is a kind of extract of the greater unseen activities of the 'greater picture' of the world. The following chapters will develop this by introducing exercises for gathering further insights. The exercise described in the previous paragraph helps us towards this impression.

The kind person who talked to their flowers spontaneously created an 'elementary' heart link to this being, which, in an elementary way, would respond. Consequentially, this must be a *life*-process that does not go into words but manifests thereby a greater degree of vitality and hence beauty. Plants acquire 'the look of flowers that are looked at'.

There is a wealth of material in Anthroposophy about all this: how the kingdoms of nature arise, how beings of an unseen world are active, according to their various kinds, in bringing plants into being. It describes how the elements of Nature work in different substances and in the traditional elements of Earth (all that is solid), Air (all that breathes), Fire (the heat that permeates everything as an entity of itself rather than as a 'property of matter') and Water (all that flows). Out of this one can speak of 'elemental' beings as those that typically 'are' the processes within the one or other of these elements, mediating between them; and some of these processes are more 'elementary' that others. This is very different from referring to something pantheistic or animistic. It is merely calling something that *is*, a being, so we know what we are talking about. 'Elemental' means here, 'of the elements'. These beings are also called 'elementary' beings because they emerge out of a particular *element*, using it for their 'body'. Later, at the end of their term of activity, they dissolve back into the element from which they came. But they, like us, are not only their body; they have a soul too, although an 'elemental one', not backed up by an ego or animal- or group-soul that would represent a more permanent existence, as that would be in the spiritual world (see R. Druitt, *Festivals of the Year*).

Nothing beyond the senses is being postulated until it is experienced. Thus the being of a waterfall is a being of the element of water, whose nature is of constant transformation, reaching into neighbouring elements of rock, air and light. The being of a plant, having a sort of watery parentage because it is alive and consists mostly of water, also has elements of the earthy and airy in it. One could say it has an 'inside' that is of earth and water, manifesting in root and leaf, and an 'outside' of air and fire, manifesting in blossom and fruit; but one would need to add that the beings of water and air work together in photosynthesis, of air and fire in pollination and of water and earth in germinating. Furthermore, one can sense that the water being of a waterfall has more duration i.e. lasts longer in time, than that of a plant, more comparable to trees that (as an Eastern consciousness perceives) acquire a Being once they reach a sufficient age to become a 'someone'. Here, however, we may not slip into anthropomorphic fantasy. This is a scientific approach where observations are made, the resultant feelings noted and followed to make more observations so that ideas and concepts of the things one observes arise out of *them* instead of being taken from elsewhere and pasted on to them. By this method of exploring the world we develop an ever-increasing inner world of interlocking picture-ideas that convince us out of their own nature that is at the same time the nature of the world, because we have added nothing to it out of thought-out theories.

To conceive these activities in one living whole will enable us, without clairvoyance, to perceive the 'plant being' in our own soul, in an enhanced thought-life. Observing a plant out of this greater picture and through the enhanced thinking we shall have gone through we perceive the *elemental being of that particular plant*. This is an imaginative, artistic thought, yet 'in' the plant as well.

This contrast between mineral and plant shows that the plant nature is an enhancement of the mineral world yet is forever grounded upon it. Actually, the mineral world is 'descended' from the plant. There are similar relationships between the animal kingdom and the two lower ones and finally between Man and the three. There is a folk image that depicts this, albeit from the animal world, the *Town Musicians of Bremen* (Brothers Grimm). Briefly summarising and interpreting: the rooster (ego) stands on the cat (soul) who in turn stands on the dog (life), then upon the ass (physical). In the story, these four, once they have become constituted as a foursome, act as *one being* to achieve their aims. Thus does each kingdom bear upon the lower ones, owing its extra freedom to their forgoing of it. Ultimately, in the *human* being, we have a nature that can self-reflect and act upon its lower parts. In this, we are at the pinnacle of creation, an idea that continues throughout this work.

Thus, when we first set eyes on a plant, that being is drawn into a kind of limbo because it has, so to speak, been enchanted into the plant by the laws of the cosmos and now begins to be released.[*] Now the human being has, through the process described above, the potential to change its destiny for better or worse. Anthropomorphically, one would say the being 'hopes' something of us when we look at it and may end up with a disappointment that gnaws away and turns to antipathy because we have failed it. Alternatively, however, we may bless it in the way another person feels, and is, blessed, when we see and appreciate them for themselves. I hope through this comparison one can see in what way this anthropomorphism is meant since our earthly language is not fitted for spiritual descriptions unless used to build pictures that have a spiritual content and that can become windows for the world beyond. If we now carefully transpose that personal feeling into a universal spiritual one, we might sense how the plant being is *elementarily* the representative of the total world in which mankind lives. Within Nature its spirit acts as a 'projection' of the universal spiritual order into our personal realm of experience.

This too can gradually acquire more transparency year by year, especially when a few of the same plant species are observed regularly. A new kind of knowing develops, a familiarity, despite the fact that one has not seen that particular plant before, only its species.

The plant being is thus *redeemed*, meaning freed from its task as a nature being and 'promoted' to become one of the positive forces that are to be found in realms of life, where people are freely creative, pushing on to bring about the good in the world. Experiencing small miracles that help us realise some of our goals is often the gift of a redeemed elemental being. If this redemption fails, the last state becomes worse than the first

---

[*]R. Steiner, Vienna, 28 September 1923, GA 223, in English as 'Michaelmas Soul' Lecture 2, or 'Michaelmas and the Soul Forces of Man'.

(Matthew: 12, 45) and the spirit becomes an epidemic or crowd panic, or a materialistic or nihilistic idea in someone's mind. Where something unimaginably terrible is reported in the media, it is sometimes only possible to grasp its horror and totally alien quality through the process here described. Later we shall look further into this process of redemption.

Our work in observation can thus liberate a freshly created force of good into the world.

2
A LEAF EXERCISE

We now begin the exercises for realising the prospects of the previous chapter: to develop our powers of observation, thinking and feeling so they can touch into those parts of the plant's makeup that are beyond perception through the senses.

This first exercise takes about an hour to do thoroughly (but is worth the effort!), so do plan ahead to avoid hurry or interruption. Switch off any background music—your own mind will be the background. You may want to study this exercise and sleep on it before starting.

Choose three fresh leaves, fairly plain simple ones, without studying them closely. Put them to one side, one, two, three, so that they can be located again just by touch.

Prepare a pencil and plain paper for the task.

Adjust to the silence, take one of the leaves and place it on the paper and study it gently for a few minutes. Then sharpen your gaze and go all over and around this leaf describing it to yourself in as much detail as you can. If you find yourself using the phrase, 'it is like', look again at that detail and ask, 'Why is it like . . . ?'; then describe it *without* comparison, in terms of line, curvature, texture, gloss and so on; concave here, convex there.

When this is complete, put the leaf aside and reconstruct it before your mind's eye, using all the detail that has been observed. Try and do this actively for half a minute, then hold it there quietly to complete the minute.

Next, draw the leaf on your paper, from your mind not from life, then close your eyes for another while. Still holding the image, pick up the same leaf again and look at it once more.

Try to register your *first impression* and *feeling*. Next put it on the page and compare it with the sketch, making any necessary corrections. What did I get wrong? What did I miss altogether?

At this point it is essential not to break the process but continue to the next step.

Put the leaf aside, let your mind rest in the experience of it so it fills the soul. After about a minute of this, close your eyes, pick up the second leaf, place it on the paper (maybe a new sheet), hold your breath a moment and in all inner stillness, ready to observe yourself, open your eyes, taking in the new leaf. Try not to think, just look and register. Let the thinking begin slowly and steadily. Take note of the sequence of thoughts, and especially any 'first impression' you may have had. This could be, for example, that one leaf has a more toothed edge than the other. Did we merely *see* it or this time also *feel* it? A potential result of spending a long time on the first one is an intensive perception like a small shock with the second. Don't worry if this makes no sense just yet: it will do in time but that time is well spent, as preparation for what comes later when we work with the plant 'Type'.

Repeat the process from the beginning as for the first leaf so that there are now two corrected sketches before you. Now try in your imagination to move forwards and backwards between these two leaves, pausing somewhere in between where your imagined leaf is no longer like the first and not yet like the second. Just try it! There is an infinitude of possibilities here just as there is in Nature. But does it not mean that our mind must be using the *same forces,* picture-building forces, to picture them as Nature does *before creating* them? The latter is something which (fortunately) *we* cannot do. Think of the chaos that would result! However, we have taken an important step into the world of life and thereby transcended the material world in our thoughts, for we have beheld and created something that does not exist in the sense world, yet using forces that do.

Our next step is to begin thinking in a *methodical* way about our observations. It is important that we stay *within our experience,* the very limited experience of the exercise so far. All other knowledge about plants is to be excluded for we want to build up our concepts from scratch. We must avoid pasting ideas on to our research until we have discovered them from within its bounds. There are only two leaves in our world: 'leaf is—these two shapes and colours.' What can we discover further about them? Ideally, try this straight away by observing them closely again and only read on after a bit of empirical research on your own. There is certain to be something that was missed (and this can go on and on throughout the years). If this is not possible just now, restart when appropriate with a recapitulation of at least one run-through of the above.

The following will sooner or later become clear: each leaf has an overall *shape,* it has a *stalk* (perhaps) and it has a smaller or greater thickening or widening at the *base.* (Between this base and the main stem can usually be seen a bud called eye or axil bud.) This is a first concept of leaf won from observation (note: by sense perception, not any apparatus) and empirical

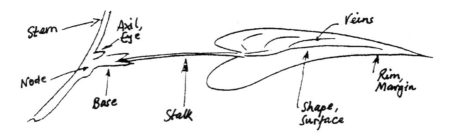

thought. A leaf is threefold—compound leaves still have a single overall shape, stalk, base and eye. The presence or absence of the eye shows the leaf to be simple or compound. We have extracted a concept out of the observed world without any hypothesis. Here our science differs again from some other: we do not use hypotheses. Instead we *identify questions* about what was actually seen. The simple *concept* won so far will guide our further observation, will quicken it. This is a contrasting method to where we would observe and think to make a *hypothesis* to explain the observation then use that hypothesis to predict another observation for which we experiment. We shall use just this method on another level later but not here. Here it is *observation* that is guided, not experimentation or the postulating of causes and certainly not explanations or definitions. We look at causation later, in the chapter on the Type.

Now take up the third leaf and observe it. The more often the exercise is performed the more will be gained—that is after all the nature of practice: it makes perfect. Then we enhance our concept of leaf accordingly. Do leaves always have a stalk, a base? Sometimes not. But they always have a shape, a Form. So that is point number one of plant observation: *a leaf has a Form*. This embraces shape, stalk and base.

It may be good to break here to refresh oneself and take stock before doing any more. The soul likes to breathe between different activities and when the exercise is later repeated or developed further, one is sure to have more vitality available for it.

The next step is to gather more leaves and examine them according to this threefold nature: shape, stalk and base. We shall find endless variety but always this common factor. Now go further and examine the different *shapes*. There are heart-shaped, spear-shaped, round and many other possibilities, all with names; each has *veins*, of differing patterns, parallel or branched (alternating, paired, radiating from the base—all too with special names) that in varying ways fill out the shape; and each has a *rim* or margin that encloses the surface. With a compound leaf the shape embraces the whole, while the rim or margin just embraces the leaf fabric of each part. We find with a compound leaf that it is the *whole* that has the base, not the parts (examples: Ash, Horse Chestnut).

Many plant books and websites devote space to all these features, shapes, venation and rims. For our purpose it is important to have the *experience* of each through observation as above, not just the knowledge 'somewhere' that they exist. As far as we can, we bring all our knowledge into our perception and bring all the fruits of perception into enhancing our concepts. This is a loose English rendering of what Goethe neatly expressed as '*denkend anschauen, anschauend denken*', literally, looking out of thinking and thinking out of looking. Thus grows our concept of Leaf, also our concept of *Form*. Each new observation is a new impression and thereby *expresses* something of the plant itself. This is the most important point in this book: to work with 'impression-expression'. It is the only way of extending our intellectual thoughts into a reality that contains *life* because an impression is more than a thought. It is therefore the only way to experience the archetypal plant, because that is something *living*. This is also the only way to experience that plants replicate their own life and growth *within our soul* when we observe them in this painstaking way. We experience again some of the spiritual access to Nature of the ancients but now in a modern way, through our thinking ego, so that we are protected from those forces of the world that would enchant us by leading us into a dreamy state where it is possible to form invalid judgements.

Once we have grasped the threefold nature of the leaf and the threefold nature of its 'shape' or 'spread' we are well equipped to guide our observation over any leaf we find. If we think about it, we know deep down that all leaves are different in form, although on reflection this seems miraculous—the discrepancy between statistical probability and Nature's bounty. But now we can experience that they are *all variations of a common idea*. We have now achieved the first step towards beholding the Archetypal Plant and its driving force, the Type. The exercises are all about gaining impressions as strongly as possible. Normal walking through the world does not usually achieve this unless some artistic training has been undergone. We are now just enhancing that process. Our leaves are all metamorphoses of this archetype and we perceived in our mental exercise that our thoughts, although lifeless in themselves, are an image of the creative force of Nature. We start to grasp the meaning of Steiner's phrase that the supersensible world is one of *thought,* in picture and in power; but that this thought is as yet only known to us as intellect.

The intellectual mode of thought has appeared gradually out of Greek thought that itself was preceded by other modes still found embodied in folk traditions like the story of the Town Musicians of Bremen, or the creation accounts of original peoples. Anthroposophy perceives and trains modes as described in this volume, that will become more widespread in the future. The virtue of the intellect is its exactness and its innocence. It lacks the magical power to change Nature that other modes have. It leaves us free to explore ideas without affecting the outer world. However, intellectual ideas do have a power to influence our thoughts; and to remain a free soul we do need to process received thoughts with our own capacities. They otherwise remain as foreign bodies in the soul and foreign bodies may not be healthy.

The next step is Metamorphosis of leaves of a single plant. We shall extend what we have learned and experienced with an array of single, independent leaves to groups of leaves that have developed together on the same stem.

3

METAMORPHOSIS

This exercise is like the previous one that explored Form, except that now it is _processes_ we shall compare rather than single objects. We observe what works _between_ one form and the next. Can we notice that we are observing something not itself sense-perceptible but '_inter_-preted' from it? Studying leaf _forms_ meant following the differences between them, building up their inherent idea, their 'metamorphosis'. We had a glimpse of metamorphosis in the previous chapter, 'somewhere in between where your imagined leaf is no longer like the first and not yet like the second'. The infinite range of potential leaf forms between the two poles of our chosen leaves is one case of metamorphosis. Now we want to compare _different_ metamorphoses with each other.

First let us observe the overall nature of the human being. One hears the formulation, 'head, heart and guts' to describe this for easy use. The head concentrates the senses and thinks; the heart beats and feels while the guts digest and give certain impressions of the imponderable. One of Rudolf Steiner's innovative contributions to a further grasp of our complex being was to point out that the head also has a feeling function manifesting in the breathing and a metabolic function in the salivary processes. The heart region has sensory and metabolic functions, for it can sense deeper realities than the normal senses and in it takes place the interchange of substance in the lungs. The guts with their outward extension of the limbs, where metabolism occurs in the muscles, clearly also has a sensory function. It senses our wellbeing but also other subtle phenomena; and it can think—e.g. where to put a finger for the next note on the keyboard. Steiner also pointed out that the head is where we grasp the spiritual while the chest is the home of the soul. The metabolism and the limbs are what deal for us with the earthly as body. It is the perceiving aspects of these three regions that is referred to in what follows.

There are two important ways of comparing metamorphoses. One is to lay all the leaves in a row and observe them as a single image then note the impression this image makes upon us, an _external_ view. The other is to study them one by one along the row as described in the last chapter, making sure we are perceiving them with the chest region (artistic) as well as the head, then close our eyes and let the overall impression register. This is the *internal* way, akin to the *impression* (a basic motif in these studies) of a melody left in us after hearing it, without us having to sing it all through in our mind. Just as we can make an intuitive comparison between two well-known melodies without needing them playing, so can we compare two different sets of leaves just by their overall impressions. Try it with *Three Blind Mice* and *The Grand Old Duke of York* for example, or anything simple you know well. The metamorphosis is not the array of leaves itself but what happens in the spaces between consecutive ones; how the leaf got from one shape to the other, or rather, how the idea of leaf that we began to discover in the last chapter works in a flow, as it were depositing various stages of this flow upon the sense-world. The series below will help clarify this. All are from the same plant. From left to right they go up the stem. As comparing different leaves helped us be aware of more detail so does the comparison of different metamorphoses attune our perception to them, whether for example they just get progressively smaller or become bigger initially then get smaller afterwards. Does the shape and proportion of each leaf remain more or less constant or do later leaves appear to be from a different plant?

We began to feel form in the chest region as an impression; now we perceive metamorphosis as a *movement* there, a kind of breathing or soundless melody.

Goethe is credited with being the first to grasp the metamorphosis of the plant, that the form of every organ is a metamorphosis of the ideal threefold leaf form. Or we can say this leaf form is the archetype for every organ in the rest of the plant. This is a simple sounding statement until one asks what it actually means. However, the spirit of the German language also knew about it, as the following vocabulary indicates. Some of these words were there in German already, before Goethe coined the rest. In either case the English language has not followed this lead, for whatever reason.

The following scheme will help clarify this view of the plant organs all being modelled on one archetypal 'leaf-type'.

Organs in their sequence up the stem, Goethe's terminology, 'Blatt' = leaf:

Key to the flower diagram below: 1 sepal, 2 petal, 3 stamen, 4 stigma, 5 ovary.

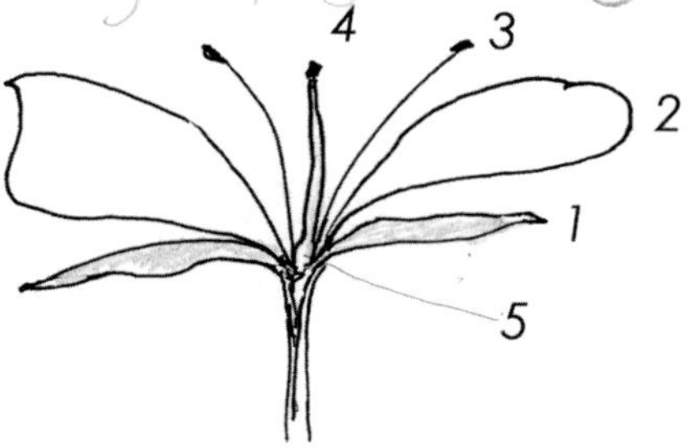

carpel: stigma, style, ovary

4   3
2
1
5

base

Keimblatt = cotyledon
Laubblatt = (foliage) leaf
Hochblatt (*Deckblatt*) = *bract*
Unterblatt = leaf base
Kelchblatt = sepal
Kronenblatt = petal
Staubblatt = stamen
Fruchtblatt = stigma

Staubblatt was previously known as Staubgefäss, *Fruchtblatt* as Stempel. The sepals make up the *calyx*, the petals the *corolla*.

In order to see how this progression works, we need to be able to grasp the leaf in its three potential parts, base (point), stalk (line) and shape or surface (plane)—see illustration in the previous chapter. Then the *base* can be followed up from the cotyledons (the pair of leaves that emerge first from the seed) into sepal and then stigma (sitting at the top of the carpel = stigma, style and ovary). The *plane* can then be followed into petal and stamen, those organs that reach out away from the stem. Goethe noted that the first group were attached to the stem, the plant's *central* organ that reveals the line from the centre of the Earth to the sphere of the Sun (rather than the actual sun in the sky). He said, 'It should be noticed that the system of calyx, corolla and stamens corresponds to the system of the stem leaves, whilst pistil, ovary and fruit belong to the system of the eyes (axil buds). Whoever can see this has taken a profound gaze into the secrets of nature.'

A modern writer, however, thinks that as modern research finds no trace of the attributes of pollen in the leaves, Goethe's, and our, view of this important polarity and metamorphosis, is not completely true. It is said by that writer that the properties of pollen come from 'above'; but that is just our point: the blossom 'descends', along with the form principle generally, and meets the stream of matter carried up by life forces from below. Goethe was aware of more than he wrote and it is a pity when modern discoveries are used to falsify his findings before he has been properly grasped. This will become clearer towards the end of the chapter.

This is an important polarity, as the centre of the Earth is the point centre of *our own* cosmos, meaning that that is our innate orientation in life, before we learn about the Earth going around the Sun.

To see what is meant by the 'sphere of the Sun', imagine the following. The astronomical sun makes an apparent path around the earth on a line called the ecliptic. It does not make loops on this path as do the planets but progresses with the steadiness required of a central organ of the universe. The sun sphere is the sphere created by rotating this round line about the sun-earth axis, as though rotating a hoop around two opposite points on its rim. This sphere breathes in and out on an annual basis because of the earth's elliptical orbit, upon which the distance between sun and earth increases and decreases each year. The hoop is not quite round. By thinking of this *sphere* rather the sun as a point in the sky we see that we are actually inside the sun, at its centre. When we now look at a flower, this centre is made manifest as an image of it. It manifests wherever something earthly works together with something spiritual. According to inspired tradition, the sun-sphere is where the Earth stops and the soul-heaven begins (a higher heaven begins outside the Saturn-sphere and a still higher one beyond the Zodiac). One can underpin such statements with observations and thoughts in the same way that the objective feeling perceptions we have made about metamorphosis are underpinned by the work done on individual leaves. The sun-sphere also has a negative pressure or suction that draws things away from the earth. Sometimes too much sun on our head draws attention to this.

The Sun sphere is thus the periphery of this cosmos of the plant. It is also the key to grasping the plant as *the* being that represents the *life* of the Solar System, its own 'personal' space being an image of the cosmos. That line from the centre of the earth that runs radially through so many plant stems is the vertical axis of the plant, giving us the name 'vertical' for the central organs as opposed to the spiral organs arranged up the stem and reaching towards the periphery (eg the leaves and stamens). Central/peripheral and central/spiral are two related ways of grouping the plant's organs. The placing of the leaves on the stem ('nutation') imitates certain planetary movements and creates the different angles the leaves make with each other as they extend outwards from it (generally 180°, 120°, 90° or 72°). The blossom, on the other hand, gives us an image of the sun, right in the centre. (Where blossoms appear to be to the side, an exact scrutiny will reveal that they are actually at the centre, the *end* of a stem, even if but a side-stem.) These reach blossoming more quickly than the main stem and make a wonderful challenge. Good plants to try this on are buttercups and blackberries, as well as roses. The division into centre and

periphery that came about at germination as the plant prepared to leave its
bed of earth is reunited in pollination. This leads to the formation of the
seed away from the earth, in the sun sphere of the flower but already
moving in a downward direction, into the inside of the plant, towards the
earth, into which it later falls, completing its full cycle from seed to seed.

Central and peripheral distinguish the variations of the leaf base and
surface in other organs of the plant while vertical and spiral indicate the
gestures and functions within the whole plant. The development of the
leaf base, a central organ, lies with the vertical while that of the surface, a
peripheral organ, with the spiral.

The four kinds of being of the elements are indicated in the picture (see
p. 22) with traditional imagery. This is not at all how they are to be
imagined. Earth element: *gnome*; water element: *undine*; air element: *sylph*
(fairy); fire element: fire spirit, traditionally called *salamander* (represented
by a bee). Dynamis and Kyriotetes refer to the spiritual beings active in the
planetary system and in laws of Nature.

Some additional exercises:

1 Try sorting a random collection of leaves of different kinds into an
order, seeing what options there are, each using a different characteristic as criterion, so that several possible sequences (hence also
metamorphoses) result.
2 Try sorting a leaf sequence (from a single stem) that has been
shuffled.

This may be a difficult chapter to grasp without a couple of plants at
hand to which to relate. Do work at it like a Latin Grammar: step by
step! Then all will be well.

★   ★   ★

Look again at the leaf in its three parts and take note of the different
quality between the leaf base and its surface. Typically, the base is thicker
and less formed and it may to some degree enwrap the stem ('stem' is used
for the main stem upon which the leaves grow and 'stalk' for the part of
the leaf connecting the base and the surface) and may be more reddish.
The surface on the other hand is generally greener and more complex.

Before looking in more detail at each single leaf, let us look at the main
stem. In annual plants (ones that have grown from a seed and will die at
the end of the season) this is the stem that has grown out of the growth
point seated between the two cotyledons, the first leaves appearing after

germination. The majority of plants are classed in one of two groups: rose type and lily type. This work will, for the sake of simplicity, deal with the rose type, dicotyledons or having two cotyledons. The lilies (grasses, bulbs etc.), monocotyledons, can be examined in similar ways but the main particulars can be illustrated without them.

Thus far, we have looked at the metamorphosis of our three-fold leaf, base-stalk-surface/spread. We shall now enhance this with a further relationship.

The rose type, which contains many, many more classes than just roses, has its leaves arranged in spirals or pairs, or else alternating, set at varying distances above one another at thickenings of the stem called nodes. There is thus i) a section of stem, ii) a node, iii) a leaf and iv) a bud (eye or axil bud, the 'growth point') between the leaf base and the stem.

We now add to our threefold leaf–form with its threefold shape (shape, margin and veins) a *fourfold* arrangement on the stem: stem, node, leaf, bud. *And this series repeats itself as we progress up the stem.* These four features are always there as long as there are leaves. By defining a leaf as that which grows at a node and has a bud in its axil, we need to call any leaf that has parts without the contained bud *compound* ones. The parts do not undergo metamorphosis in the same way as the whole leaf; and it is the whole leaf in the sense we define it that brings out the secrets of the plant's nature as it undergoes metamorphosis.

Referring to the sequence depicted above, it is seen that as the leaves unfold further up the stem (going towards the right in the illustration), their surface changes in size and complexity. Often the rim and any larger indentations change. The way this happens is an important part of the form that is observed in its metamorphosis. It is generally to be found that this increases in size then stops and reverses. It should be noted whether the base also changes as this varies from species to species, from negligible (rose, dock) to extreme (sow thistle, cow parsley). At the same time, the internode (the distance between successive nodes) increases and decreases as well, though not necessarily synchronously. Then comes a point where only a small, in many cases narrow, organ appears in place of the leaf: the bract. There may be a number of these. This is the moment in following the metamorphosis when we hold our breath to take in this progressive shrinking of the leaves into pointed narrow forms; for then out of this nothingness appears the bud. *Becoming,* or inwardly identifying with, the leaf in its growing helps *experience* the contraction (of life held back) that becomes the flower bud. Watch for the feeling of beholding something from another world that has descended on to the plant stem from the light above (the sun sphere referred to before), like an inner sunrise. The more

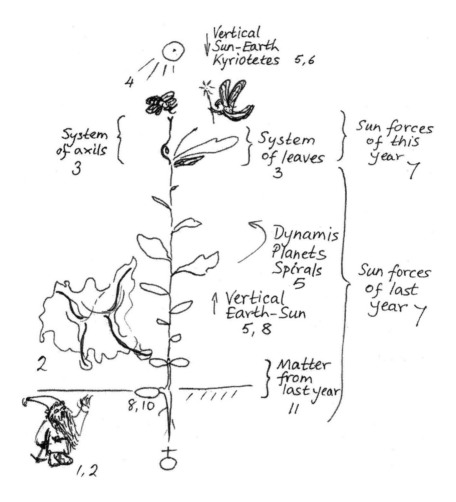

Vertical
Sun-Earth
Kyriotetes   5,6

4

System
of axils
3

System
of leaves
3

Sun forces
of this
year

Dynamis
Planets
Spirals
5

Vertical
Earth-Sun
5, 8

Sun forces
of last
year

2

Matter
from
last year
11

8,10

1, 2

Key to Diagram

1 GA 230 Man as Harmony of the Creative Word, Lecture 7: elemental beings in plant reproduction; seed as male principle rather than pollen, Earth as female principle rather than stigma respectively.

2 GA 223 Anthroposophy and the Human *Gemüt*/The Michaelmas-Soul, Lecture 2: the liberation of the plant spirit through the right human gaze.

3 Goethe's *Natural Scientific Writings Vol 5*, 'Prose Aphorisms': whoever can perceive that sepal, stigma and ovary belong to the system of the axil buds and that leaf blade, petal and stamen to the system of stem leaves has attained a deep insight into Nature's secrets.

4 GA 99 Theosophy of the Rosicrucian, Lecture 4, divine-spiritual forces work on plants.

5 GA 136 The Spiritual Beings in the Heavenly Bodies and the Kingdoms of Nature, Lecture 9: Vertical and Spiral tendencies and the union of Sun and Planets

6 GA 143 The Mysteries of the Kingdom of Heaven ... Cologne, Lecture 7.5.12, *The Calendar of the Soul* (two-thirds through): leaves on the stem follow the spirals of the planets.

7 GA 219 Man and the World of the Stars, Lecture 8: 'up to the blossom the plant derives from the preceding year'.

8 GA 28 *The Course of My Life*, Chap. VI: the plant as a sequence of forms, each arising out of the previous one.

9 GA 10 *How is Knowledge of Higher Worlds attained?* 'Preparation'. The right attitude for observation. See Introduction.

10 GA 1 Goethe's *Natural Scientific Writings*. Chap IV, The ripened seed as 'sum' of the plant, the seed in the ground its 'result': 'Concept as the *sum* of experience, the Idea its *result*.'

11 GA 123 The Gospel of St Matthew, Lecture 11: this year's plant is of new matter/substance, without genetic material from last year.

we do this exercise, the more the feeling develops of being 'inside' the plant, shrinking with one's chest region as the leaf shrinks. Then we 'know' that the flower comes from outside whilst an external view cannot see this. As mentioned, metamorphosis is not perceived by the senses: they only perceive single leaves; but the mind and heart can see the metamorphosis and open the way for these sensations to become, through practice, *exact feeling perceptions*. They are exact because their basis in an enhancement of mental activity enables them to be explained, while 'mere' feelings or even intuitions often cannot be and must therefore rank as subjective. It is a wonderful emancipation to discover that our feelings, though possibly the most intimate part of our soul, that are definitely subjective, can be trained *in partnership with thinking* to be objective. Thinking is brought to life by feeling; feeling is objectified by thinking. Wonderful! Art and science in partnership.

Once above the bracts we are looking up at the bud from below, from the earthly, and seeing its composition: the star of sepals, generally the same colour and texture as the leaf base! Within it is held the corolla, full of colour; 'colour' in contrast to 'green'. The petals sit in a flattened spiral with the sun inside them like a throne upon which other organs are visible. Scientific nonsense but an artistic reality. Let us think it through. After the contraction into the bud, a new *expansion* begins, into the petals. The leaf we began to know so well has separated out into two parts. The base has become sepal, the surface petal, and the stalk has vanished. We see the bract then in a new light, not now as a separate organ of its own but one caught between leaf and sepal, with minimal spread and still the same base. The sepals proper may indeed still retain hints of the spread but are largely 'base' organs, under the influence of the central principle, while the petals proper, especially the outer ones, will show traces of leaf. This is a very special area of the plant to explore: on the one hand there is a continuous progression through all the organs; on the other we see that the polarity of leaf base and surface continues into sepal and petal.

But development does not stop there. We had followed the expansion of the leaves from the cotyledons and their *contraction* into the bud. Now we journey through the expansion of the petals then their contraction into the centre of the 'sun-sphere'. Here are to be found the stamens around the stigma, right in the centre—the uppermost organ of the centre or vertical axis. This vertical aspect of the plant was looked at above. We are engaged with it directly at this point since the foliage has simplified itself and re-emerged on a more sublime level in the blossom. Here there is another expansion and contraction: pollen is released and although it may only need to go a millimetre, it may nonetheless travel long distances before it reaches a stigma (pollen grains have been found high up in the earth's atmosphere). The petals and sepals are separated morphologically (i.e. according to form) from each other (in the leaf they were joined by the stalk). The anthers, or pollen bearing part of the stamen, let free their pollen to separate from the plant *altogether*. The expression 'peripheral organ' here reaches its culmination as the pollen flies far (into the sun sphere) to gather the warmth needed for begetting a new plant when it unites with the earth, carried there by the seed.

The gesture of pollination therefore is a downward one, qualitatively embracing half the solar system before reaching the central point of the stigma where the force it has acquired (from the sun) stimulates a further expansion and contraction, this time in the downward direction within the central organs of style and ovary. The ovary expands, perhaps as fruit, vegetable or nut and within it there is a contraction into seed or germ. The seed thus 'is' a distillation of the cosmos through the archetypal plant that quickens the part of the uplifted earth that the ovary represents. When the seed then falls to earth, heaven and earth are united. This observation of the plant from seed to seed indicates that the final seed is an outcome of the metamorphosis: it is its gesture but as a point. The Earth conceives by the power of the Sun. The world of plants manifests this life of the earth.

With this turning downwards or inwards, the growth also stops (except rarely: Goethe had found a rose that continued growing up through the blossom). The side-growth takes over until it too reaches blossoming, which is generally much sooner than the main growth. This means more spreading of the blossoming and accounts for the final shape of trees, as described in Chapter 9, 'Bare Trees in January'. The tree reaches in this way a satisfying shape around which the atmosphere is different. The scent of nectar attracts insects and the whole tree can be enclosed in a sphere of sun-activity. This is one of the places where mutations can occur, for it is a gap in the plant's being that is closed with pollination. External influences, human or spiritual, can be applied there. The other gap is in the time between the seed reaching the earth and its germination, where plant breeders make their selections.

Again, it must be remarked that this is not an alternative to science but an enhancement of it, not unlike the difference between knowing a pen friend and the human relationship that can come about once met. We can well study the growth of plants through cellular division and so on; but we can go further—and are trying to do so—to the line between sun and earth and the spiralling movements of the planets. Anthroposophy might say, 'The true being of the plant is revealed in this dual activity between ascent and descent in the vertical or earth-sun axis (the central organs as expression of individuality) and the planetary spiralling, looping movements, that bring variation of a life-soul character within the species.'

Our next step will be into the realm of *Gesture*, grasped as a further enhancement of thoughtful observation in its artistic mode, a further development of that from Form to Metamorphosis.

4

WHAT AM I SEEING WHEN I LOOK?

A self-correcting path to knowing

When I open my eyes I see first a profusion of colour, then, almost simultaneously, pick out shapes. Usually without effort, I recognise and perhaps subconsciously name them; then I can move on to my next task in the day. But what really happens when I notice shape? My eye is travelling inadvertently along lines where different colours meet and this movement is interpreted as a form. Something other than sight is acting, for sight only perceives the colour. *Form* therefore is already a fruit of co-operation of more than one sense: that of sight (colour) and of movement (line). With hearing too, it must be a sense of movement that informs us of a musical interval or of a word. Different senses may work together like this to provide us with the sensation of *world*, but each single sense has its fundamental perception: the sense of sight is colour (with light/dark); the sense of hearing is an isolated sound and so on. It is not usual to call colour by itself 'form' but for the sake of the methods of this book I would like to do so here. We shall call *the fundamental sensation of every* sense 'form', even if it requires the assistance of another sense to give us a perception of *a* form.

The work done by this second sense leads us beyond perception into *mental activity*, but to remain honest in the realm of perception, concentration is needed to hold off this need to comprehend, otherwise our perception is intermixed with thought. We have struggled to achieve this ability as infants but now we must struggle to hold it at bay to rediscover pure perception, the sensation that is *purely* of sense, nothing else. We shall call this the 'pure perception' and the impression it makes upon us the 'pure experience', two important steps before the forming of the 'mental picture' that is gradually progressed to becoming a concept, then an idea.

1 Pure Perception = what a sense organ perceives without mental activity coming into play
2 Pure Experience = the impression this makes on us before we think about it

3 Mental-Picture = the image we build in our mind of our sense perception, again without thought activity
4 Thought-Picture = this picture with thought description added
5 Concept = the thought without the picture, based on several related thought-pictures
6 Idea = a higher order of concept embracing a number of related concepts

Note: Mental-Picture and Thought-Picture are usually combined as 'Mental-Picture' but here it is helpful to separate them, since it is important to be conscious of the action of thought in mental imagery when dealing with our perceptions in the sense world.

Picking up at point 3, Mental-Picture, recall the later exercise in Chapter 3 that introduced *metamorphosis*, where we took the mental-pictures of two different leaves and explored the mind space that mysteriously lies between them. We ask now, 'From where comes the content of this space?'; for we saw there a range of leaf images created in our mind as we adjusted the feature of one leaf to become more like the other.

How did we do that, creating images that we have never seen? In dreams we are able to imagine whole scenes with people dressed perfectly. It took no time at all for our soul to achieve this, yet either we have designed these clothes ourselves or had the ability to choose them spontaneously from the forgotten images of people we once saw. Dreaming comes about as our soul's night-boat crosses the shoals on its way back to the shore of the body. The ocean of our life body throws up an infinitude of images for our soul to render into its own story, sometimes prophetically. Now our soul, the mind part of it, can select the image it wants to use out of the infinitude of Nature. The concentration brought to bear on the exercise taps us in to the life body of the Earth, where the pictures live, in an endless flow of form-changing. We can now speak of *metamorphosis* (Greek; Latin = transformation); it is a different level of perception from that of form but just as exact. It requires more effort to achieve: but then at last we 'see' it. We see it with our mind but by using our mind in an unusual way, although there are common examples like perceiving the meaning of a word or the quality of a melody instead of a sequence of sounds, which we carry out largely automatically. Thus we ourselves can find the content of this space between the two leaves, within the life body of the Earth, analogous to our own memory bringing up images from our own life body.

So what else am I seeing when I look?

The exercises with leaves of Chapter 3 onwards observe the *sequence* of leaves that belong together (from the same plant). We notice that the creation of *form* reaches nearer to the sensory realm than that of metamorphosis and that by working with *metamorphosis* we are penetrating through the sense world a step deeper. By looking at metamorphosis we see below the surface, although *below* is not meant spatially. So, what is it that is there?

In Chapter 1 we opened the theme of elementary beings and the spirits of plants but besides describing these beings of Nature, Anthroposophy describes higher beings that bring forth the sense world out of the spirit. These are creator spirits and here we can refer to Genesis, where creation is instituted by the Elohim or, in the New Testament, Exusiae, Greek for the ones who can place 'being' (*ousia*) *outside* (ex) themselves. Jahweh (Jehovah) as creator spirit is one of the seven primary Exusiae that worked together to create Man (see Genesis), hence the plural 'let *us* make Man'; and just before that we have the phrase 'the Lord God', i.e. 'Jahwe Elohim', Jahwe (singular) the Elohim (plural): Jahwe the one amongst and together with the choir of Elohim, but all acting as one. Note, this is not yet 'God the Father'; for this work we are not going higher than the spirit beings referred to in this chapter.

Behind these great beings others are active: the Spirits of Movement and hence metamorphosis. They can be imagined as belonging to the heavenly realm beyond that of the Sun. What they create is far beyond our sight but able to be divined in *seeing* metamorphosis. We tried to grasp metamorphoses of different plants to gain an impression of their *typical* nature, to get to know them in general. When we then look at an *individual* plant we not only see its species through its *leaf* but also through its *metamorphosis*. We 'know' it on a higher level and can 'see' its idiosyncrasies by comparison with the generic image we have built up in our soul. This gives us the higher mental connection to that plant described in the chapter 'Looking at Flowers'. Anthroposophy describes these Spirits of Motion (Dynamis) as the ones that bring a metamorphosis 'down' towards the sense world from higher realms that are nearer to the source of all being and give it over to the Spirits of *Form* who will bring it into sense-perceptibility, into outer form. By studying forms and raising sense perception by mental activity to their metamorphosis, we reach back up to the level of these Spirits of Motion and can have the beginnings of an inner *experience* wherein, at its core, lies a truth. This is not an article of faith *but a more refined form of sensation that takes place in our mind.* Remembering the effort to 'see' something between our two leaf pictures, we now believe ourselves to be in possession of reality. We suggest that this sensed reality is connected to these Spirits of Motion, a kind of projection of their lofty being into our own modest horizon, a very remote foretaste of spiritual perception.

We can forever check its validity because we have authority over what takes place in our mind—or can acquire it with practice. 'Authority' contains the word author and does not only mean a writer, but someone who creates out of his own essential being. The word is used for God in this sense and derives from the Greek, an emphatic form of he, she or it and means something that exists out of itself, *autos*. This is an idea that transcends all religious ideas about God or not God. If one can think it, it is its own proof.

When we survey something inwardly with our thinking and monitor this consciously, we can often spot the inevitable gap in our knowing. That is what is meant by 'using our inherent authority' because we have used a self-reflective self-consciousness. These are many words but needed for a very important point for humanity and its contrast with the animal kingdom. It is no use saying that all this is *subjective,* because thinking has a capacity, easy to discover, of dissolving away what we notice *is* subjective and gradually raising the content of our mind to ever greater *objectivity.* 'Ever greater' because it is a process where each league trodden reveals another ahead that was not seen before. This runs parallel, as the present discourse can show, to reaching further 'up' from the sense world and discovering that the world of thinking is at the same time the world of the spirit. Touching the realm of the Spirits of Motion begins to open for us the world of *movement*, which, in Chapter 12, we shall find to be the main characteristic of ensouled beings, the animals (*anima* = breath, hence *soul*). To reach the main characteristic of *plants* we must scale higher, into the realm of the Spirits of *Wisdom*, expressed in the relationship between Sun and Earth manifest in the plant stem, described in the previous chapter.[*]

This is grasped in the next dimension of observation, *Gesture*. We now have as overview:

1 Everyday Perception—sense organs—the human realm—*Form*—
   Spirits of Form
2 Artistic Perception—chest region—animal kingdom—*Metamor-*
   phosis—Spirits of Motion

---

[*] Reference: Rudolf Steiner, *The Spiritual Beings in the Heavenly Bodies and the Kingdoms of Nature*, CE/GA 136.

3 Sculptural Perception—limb and gut regions—plant kingdom—
  Gesture—Spirits of Wisdom

We need not accept as 'revelation', although a surprising number of
people do, people's clairvoyant or sensitive utterances about beings of
Nature and the angelic world. We may use the opportunity to learn
something from them, especially if we follow them with thought, taking
care to avoid any nebulous mysticism. This is using our 'authority' in the
sense just described; then we find our way there and independently
through observation and thinking. We grow *with* the object, or 'subject
matter' and let it replicate itself within us. Thinking as a *faculty* here grows
together with thinking as *content*. The subject/object schism is overcome,
hence that of subjective/objective as well. It 'feels' (and is) more secure
than adopting the statements of others. To share anything sensitive of my
own world I would need to express it in verifiable steps like a travel guide
so that others could follow, or at least 'watch the video' and make a
thinking assessment (rather than judgement) based on their own
experience. I need to present material so that others can access it upon
their *own* 'authority'.

'Gesture' then is the leitmotif for plant observation. How do we reach
it? We took two leaf forms and examined what weaves dynamically in the
realm between them. What now if we take two metamorphoses with
which we have become familiar (that is why the exercises need doing over
time to bear fruit) and look at what is between *them*; try with our mind to
move from the one to the other and back again? If you begin to feel at this
point that we have left behind normalcy, you are right. But that is now
exactly what we need to do. The step from form to metamorphosis was a
challenge but not really out of the ordinary. We had the familiar example
of a melody to demonstrate metamorphosis. Gesture we think of merely
as dramatic gesture; but now we want to reach a clear stage further away
from the sense world to find the projection of the lofty Spirits of Wisdom
into our everyday, familiar world, our world of gesture.

Picture a series of, say, rose leaves, with their simple start at the bottom
of the stem. They become more complex the further up we go. Then,
near the bud, appear organs that remind us of the rudimentary first leaves
yet with the base developed instead of the tip! Compare this now with
leaves of a tree. In general they show little variation of *shape* in the series of
leaves up one stem (they may vary in size). They certainly do not go
through the development of shape that a rose leaf does but there *is* still
metamorphosis, even if less 'exciting' than the rose, and finally there is the

big jump in form between the foliage and the blossoms. We have before us two different metamorphoses: the one varied but cohesive, the other in two almost distinct parts.

But less exciting may mean more stable. Anthropomorphically, they may make a good partner for the more sanguine of us who need something steady in the background. But can you sense the kind of perception that can come out of this? The one metamorphosis is crowned by a striking blossom; the other bears the quality of the steady, reliable rotation of the stars! Thus can metamorphosis be 'read'; that is Gesture.

As we became more awake to leaf forms via contrast, so too do we awaken to metamorphosis; and as leaf contrast awakens us to metamorphosis, so does comparison of metamorphoses awaken us to the *gesture* of each.

'Gesture' is the word for this 'something' that appears *between* metamorphoses and throws light on each one of them. It captures succinctly their essential quality. Because it *impresses* us, it must be *expressing* something of its inner nature. There can be no seal impressed without the die that expresses it.

We receive an impression, even a gentle one like the edge of a leaf. When we really receive it deeply, as repeated practice helps us to do, it is like another kind of perception, for we are taking in more than its superficial qualities and are *struck* by what it *expresses* of itself. That is not yet the inner being. That will come later; but *expression* is an indication of *something that expresses*. We have an *impression*; we read an *expression* from it; we infer a *being* that is making the expression, a being whose expression it *is*.

We grasped gesture intuitively even on the level of *form*; but the gesture we grasp going through the hard imaginative work of 'interpreting' *metamorphoses* is more articulate. Just as a metamorphosis has transcended the sense world—hence is 'supersensible' or at least intuitive—so gesture is a perception higher still, as it also transcends the level of the Spirts of Movement. Anthroposophy describes this as the realm of the Spirits of *Wisdom* who take a divine thought and draw out of it its inner being which they clothe in gestures. People have their gestures—they unwittingly portray themselves thereby. Some gestures run in families, others are our own. Some are of face and hands, others of posture. Some change with our inner growth, others remain stubbornly fixed to us. Likewise with plants: some belong to the species, some to the individual. They all reveal the hidden wisdom of that being. That means that the Being, the kernel, is clothed or sheathed on its way towards the sense world; and that first sheath is called wisdom because it gives to the being its sense, what it is going to do and how it is going to be. This also suggests that the spirit of plants is still in the hands of the greater cosmos whereas ours is in our own hands.

With gesture we have come very close to the being itself. Form is the essence of the mineral kingdom and our mineral body; metamorphosis is the essence of the plant kingdom and our vital (etheric) body, and gesture is the essence of the animal kingdom. The way animals move about is an expression of their feeling, even though their movements are determined by their physical body, whereas Man can make movement that transcends the limitations of his body and temperament. Finally, our soul and self build the essence of the Human kingdom, i.e. our ego or spirit. This, our human structure, is worked out in Rudolf Steiner's book, *Theosophy*, section 'The Essential Nature of Man'.

Our soul is revealed in the way we move around in life, in our actions, feelings and thoughts; and here we are in the company of animals. To belong to the human kingdom as well as the animal one means to take hold of our thinking in our thought processes, and lead them consciously up the path here described. 'Morality' used to mean following the rules of our religion and society, rules given in and for earlier times, generally still valid for people who live together, between Nature and 'God' today. However, when we bring up children, there is a first stage where we have to be in control. Children need to learn from this in order to become their own author later and we may worry if young people stay at this stage without rebellion against it. Does not morality nowadays ask more of us than being good in the context of the rules? It is widely accepted both in law and in society that there can be extenuating circumstances, where laws need to be broken: from jumping the lights to make way from an ambulance to the serious questions around using modern medical techniques to change destinies. Developing our *own* sense of morality belongs to being a modern human being. This is done through the ego as the term is used here and in the next chapter. The grasping of Gesture, leading as it does to a deeper appreciation of things and people, is a valuable tool for this.

Continuing the way described above with Jahwe, this way of looking at the plant lets us enter the workshop of the beings that make up the Second Hierarchy: Exusiae, Dynamis and Kyriotetes. This is the *middle* rank of spiritual hierarchies, connected with the Sun as it governs our Solar System. Below it is the Third Hierarchy, nearest to the human being, consisting of those angelic beings caring for life and the future of ourselves (Angels), our nation (Archangels) and the world as a whole (Archai). The Second Hierarchy, being considered here, bears the laws manifest in the *forms* of the planets as heavenly bodies, in their *movements* (as seen with the naked eye, with their paths and loops) and their *gestures* or cosmic script that the Magi and other initiates could read. Going further, this Second Hierarchy is in turn just below a First Hierarchy, Seraphim, Cherubim and Thrones, the mighty beings manifest in the fabric of the sense world: colour, texture and tone, gently in thunder and lightning, devastatingly in the tearing apart of matter in a nuclear explosion respectively. We meet here the fabric of creation, which is then rendered perceptible through the natural laws that reveal the work of the Second Hierarchy. Before this wide and lofty perspective it may be clearer what effort is required to reach from the familiar plant into the realm of creation. This work is intended to aid this effort. Some further thoughts about it are formed in what follows.

When we *look*, in a particular way, we see the living work of mighty beings that have placed the fabric of substance for other beings to render as the Kingdoms of Nature, helped by the Beings of the Elements who work there but also help us in our efforts to look, and *see*.

5

GESTURE

The last chapter made the connection from plant observation to certain spiritual beings connected with Nature and introduced the perception of Gesture as an aid to sensing their activities. Here we develop the theme further with plants themselves.

Speaking in public reveals our gestures and these remain unconscious until we learn to master them, using them creatively and purposefully rather than just letting them be. This is because as human beings we live on this threshold between being all too human, part of Nature, with idiosyncratic gestures, and being creative individuals able to stand over against Nature, particularly our own, changing natures for the better and leading them on creatively. We described this earlier while 'Looking at Flowers'.

The impression that a movement makes on us, what it leaves us with, is a 'gesture'. Nature is rich with the gestures of moving leaves in the wind or the breeze sweeping over field or water but there is also the gesture we met in each form and in each metamorphosis, without the external agency of wind. We found that comparing and contrasting two different metamorphoses helped us perceive the gestures of each, the expression of the way the forms changed step by step up the plant, as shown in the picture in Chapter 3. Now we are meeting it on a higher level still: the individual leaf is no longer there, nor is the array of leaves that enabled us to perceive metamorphosis. We have left behind the sense world and the next level beyond it. We are in the region of manifestation of the being of the plant itself: its full Idea.

The gesture of leaf could be expansive or outgoing, aggressive, calm, delicate and so on, that of metamorphosis smooth, gradual, rhythmic, plain etc. Now we try to examine gesture as such, 'gesture of gesture'. How can we do this?

It could be experienced how the step from the single leaf, which is seen with the senses, to a series of leaves, which is not visible to the senses except where it has 'deposited' a leaf form into the sense world, required some imaginative effort. We have referred to the Spirits of Form who work behind this process from the 'place' where the metamorphosis 'lives' (beyond the senses, i.e. in a 'supersensible' world). The same was attempted then with a number of metamorphoses instead of single leaves.

Having them spread before one makes it easier to envisage; but here we are working on a higher level, a realm where everything is in flux. There are no single, static objects, only movement. This is an image of the realm of the Spirits of Motion, who bring something of the *being itself* into expression in the metamorphosis. Comparing metamorphoses helps tune our observation to notice the subtleties of what is thus revealed. This 'something' is the gesture; it is for the plant, and other features of the world of Nature, what we absorb from another person when attending to them speaking. In this case, however, it is the true manifestation of the plant being, not something they need to train or overcome, for they are nature beings, not ego-beings like us, who have a different task in the world order.

Gesture is the third stage of our observations, reaching as it does the pinnacle of Nature. As seen above, it is ever-present in the human kingdom too, where it can be changed—with much effort—by the ego-nature of the human being. It is in its *own* element in the animal kingdom, where it runs about with them, bound up with the immutable form of their bodies, whereas in plants (and minerals—see Chapter 11) it is found 'above' the metamorphosis, far from the sense world and requiring much more effort to perceive than, say, watching a large dog gallop along the beach in the face of a brisk breeze.

So, each leaf has a gesture, each series has one; what about the whole plant? It has a whole range of gestures typical to it:

> the shoot coming out of the ground
> the first leaves
> subsequent leaves
> blossoms, side-growth
> the fully grown plant; the partially, then fully, grown tree
> the way and direction the buds along a branch open into leaf stems
> relationship to light, rain, wind
> the fading plant, the dead plant
> the bare branch (developed in Chapter 9)
> colour gesture: bluebells in a field or in woodland shade, flax (blue)
>   or rapeseed (yellow) in a field, buttercups, dandelions, or daffodils
>   in a wood; these examples demonstrate where colours are at home
>   in the matrix of light and shade.

The exercise now is to make a strong mental image of each of these features, so that they live on in us not only as a mental-picture but as a *gesture*, perceived, registered in our own muscles, our limbs, our belly.

Then we bring them all together into one whole. With metamorphosis we could reverse the order (moving from the petals back through the leaves). This fructifies our 'impression'; but as a *gesture*—our task here—it is not so easy. Gesture does not have a forwards and backwards. Form was in three-dimensional space, metamorphosis in two. Gesture has really only one dimension, as a relationship between relationships, unless of course it comes 'downwards' into the sense-world, in which it appears to adopt the three-dimensionality of everything else. So, reversing gesture can only mean making a responding gesture to the 'owner' of the one we just experienced.

From a mathematical point of view, one may want to put form into a two-dimensional space since geometry lends itself to that; then metamorphosis is one-dimensional, i.e. linear. Gesture would then be but a point—non-dimensional. But Rudolf Steiner wrote a very challenging article on Goethe's conception of space (*Nature's Open Secret*, Anthroposophic Press, p183), based on relationships between sense-objects and relationships between relationships. He showed there can be no more than three dimensions. After that everything devolves upon the Idea. In our context, form is clearly in three dimensions, metamorphosis in two, gesture in one and the being itself beyond dimension, purely spiritual. As will be developed further in Chapter 11, on rocks, *gesture* is on the threshold between Nature and Spirit; Nature being organized spiritually by the Spirits of Form, Movement and Wisdom (for gesture manifests the *wisdom* of something). Spirit on the other hand is the foundation upon which all this is able to happen and at the same time the source of the seed archetypes that these beings interpret downwards/outwards to become sense-perceptible. We sometimes have a flash of vision when looking at Nature. This is a gesture of grace from that quarter towards ours, to which we may, with grace, respond.

Once the whole plant has been grasped in the above way it becomes possible to say that just as the gesture is revealed out of the metamorphosis, it is the seed that in real material terms emerges from the plant itself. It is the 'gesture' of the plant, in the material of real life. It is a physical centre for the imagination of the plant. A Sufi saying goes:

> The seed in the heart of the flower is the secret of the plant.
> Its source and its goal are not centred on the flower as it appears
> but the seed.
> The seed is the flower's beginning and its end.
> The seed is everything.

The Gospel, indicating the coming Resurrection, develops this: '*Unless a grain of wheat falls into the earth and dies, it remains alone but if it does die it bears much fruit*' (John: 12, 24). The earth embraces in its great nurturing being all seeds that fall, absorbs all gestures of the year whilst their imaginative counterparts are lifted up by the 'sun' of our appreciative gaze. Parallel to natural plant growth is the unfolding into life of the inner plant gesture that we have attained to through the exercises. Linked now to our observation of plants, their elementary beings and their redemption will be taken further along their own paths.

Later, when we look at rocks, we shall attempt to cross this threshold from Nature to Spirit to encounter the spiritual individualities there of the beings of Nature here. 'Eye to eye'—I to I. This sounds just too abstract and fanciful until we move along this path some more. The humble dandelion becomes the inspirer to behold its 'faery' who guides us towards the *idea* of mighty spiritual beings that stand behind that dandelion as the authors of natural law who make it visible. But then this Idea draws nearer to us as we work towards enlivening it within ourselves. Nature is no longer just 'out there'; she works within as the force of creation. The hidden beings begin to be felt within; the separation of *I* from *it* dissolves away. St Paul expressed it: 'Now I see as in a mirror, dimly, but then I shall see face to face' (1 Corinthians: 13,12).

It is not dissimilar between people. The inner being of the one is hidden from the other until they work back from appearances of dress and countenance, through their behavioural gesture to intuit their true self; but this is a two-way process. Someone can remain hidden from us however interested in them we may be unless we cross the threshold of our own self-interest, displacing it with interest in the other. In knowing the other, one finds oneself.

6
THE TYPE

'Typical!'

—When we say this of a person it tends to be judgemental, that they have slipped into a typecast of their ordinary nature rather than being creative and original. 'Type' means for the human being a particular category of behaviour. One can say someone is a typical Virgo or a typical Melancholic but that really means they are not being quite their full selves; for to be true to oneself means transcending these types or type-castings or inborn or acquired ways and working out of the ego or self. Building on the ideas developed in the last chapter, we might now see that this is something that distinguishes us from animals and indeed makes us into that part of Nature that can grow beyond her. This unique ego, which is different for every human being, is what makes for true idealism, inventiveness, community, morality and much more. Above all, it is the pivotal core of our being that can transform everything in us that has kinship with the other kingdoms of Nature into a higher being that is our future.

Colloquially we refer to a 'real type' to mean just this: someone who *is* original, has created their *own* 'type'. Then 'typical' can be positive and mean they have been just that: they have created something new out of themselves.

We see here the two meanings of the word *type*. In Nature it is that which governs a generation of beings as a living, formative archetype, whereas in Humanity it means the result of the individual creating something new out of themselves, something which others may even find worth emulating.

In Geology, the word occurs in the phrase 'type locality'. This is a place in the landscape where a rock feature is best represented and is so named. In England for example, on the Sussex coast between Hastings and Pett Level, there are several miles of cliff composed of clay and sandstone interlayered with a few other sorts of rock as well. One of these layers, however, that runs virtually the whole length of several miles but varies in thickness, displays a very much greater thickness at a place called Cliff End. This rock is therefore called Cliff End Sandstone; and the place Cliff End is the 'Type Locality'. This is a very modest fact in the vast realm of geology but well describes the principle. It does not necessarily mean that that stone is only found there. Portland Stone *is* only found near Portland in Dorset even though similar rock (limestone of a certain age) is found elsewhere too; but Cambrian rock is found all over the world, not just in Cambria (Wales). 'Type Locality' is very important for our study because it is somewhere we can behold a natural phenomenon *and* its name or 'concept' *together.*

Rudolf Steiner describes this: 'To see the concept in the real phenomenon is the true communion of humanity.' 'Concept' here means the thought-filled picture of a natural phenomenon created through observing and thinking about it. That is something we hold in our mind, whereas the real phenomenon is that piece of the world that we are observing at that moment. He considers seeing in this way out of thinking in this way to be a kind of communion. The object beheld becomes one with the idea that authors it. This is not to downgrade Holy Communion into something profane but elevate it to the level of a science that opens to the spirit. It does this by allowing for a special experience of the ego that goes beyond what is measurable. It suggests that thinking (seeing mentally) the *idea* of Christ's death and resurrection whilst at the same time *perceiving* it through a eucharistic service, is true communion. The word *idea* derives from a Greek word for 'to see'. 'True' here is not as opposed to false but more connected with the realm of the true, i.e. that great web of thought where every concept fits harmoniously with those around. This is illustrated in a large flock of wheeling birds, where there is an immediate sense of wholeness in a common reality. Religion is thus enhanced beyond the realm of honest devotion to that of true knowledge, into *science*, but a *transformed* science. Conversely, to see its Type as we look at a plant raises our knowing up to a scientific-*religious* level, one that *connects* us (one of the possible meanings of 'religion') to the universe as described in the chapter, 'What am I seeing . . . ?' Knowledge of this sort is fuller than plain knowledge of facts and events.

Anthroposophy, in commenting on the Nature study of Goethe, uses 'type' particularly in connection with the organic world as distinct from the inorganic (mineral), and especially for the plant kingdom. It has a hierarchy of uses: from the Archetypal Plant that contains, in a living spiritual dynamic, the *Idea* of the whole plant kingdom and is formatively active as individual plants come into being, down through genera and species. Researching the type is what we are attempting in the exercises: moving from observation of one entity to its neighbours and building up our concepts and mental imagery as we go, without adding on anything from outside. But the type is *supersensible* and not just like laws of motion that operate from *outside* the phenomena. That is why we make the effort to grasp the metamorphosis and gesture on the way to building our 'idea' of a particular plant rather than remain with just classifying its outer forms and following their chemistry. The exercises want to help us find our way into the *internal* workings of the plant as it develops. We experience something of its inner nature and we grow and change form along with it. The type is something that every single plant of a particular species has in common for it is out of the type that individual plants develop uniquely in their individual place on Earth. It is thus a kind of Plant Being. Steiner has used this expression in a public treatise on Goethe's work on metamorphosis, where he has not gone into the areas of 'plant spirituality' as we are doing in some of these chapters. One can, however, see that the Type has much to do with the plant ego, a kind of life body of it that is able to adapt to any environment.

When we looked at a single leaf, we tried to distinguish the first impact it made upon us from the thinking activity that stepped into action almost instantaneously, hiding the first 'impression' (and therefore what the leaf in its purity actually 'expressed'). This was referred to in the description of the leaf exercise. When we hold off the thinking and let this impression mark itself deeply upon whatever it is in us that registers impressions (a 'sentient' body of some kind), then look back at it in memory, that is our first stage: the 'mental-picture'. Note the sequence around this in Chapter 4. It is worth some practice to observe this whenever we are studying any plant organ and especially when we move to a comparison with other leaves. Then we go beyond shape, measure and colour to the *impact* or impression its being makes upon us. What is not allowed in one form of science is of the essence here, as we soon notice when the change becomes perceptible with our *artistic* sense *as well as* our head.

My initiation into this was as a young man in an art gallery in Italy. I had spent a long time looking at a well-built horseman of Marino Marini, whose work was new to me. Then I dreamily moved to the next gallery and was immediately struck by a standing man of Modigliani—a strikingly *thin* man! That has forever been for me a kind of 'type locality' of perceiving *gesture*. That is for me the place in the world where *gesture* is to be found in its essence. It was an experience somewhere just below the heart and lungs, which is where I believe all our truly *artistic* experiences, rather than mentally enlightening ones, are felt. This is another aspect of the threefold human being looked at briefly before. The head is the home of the intellectual and reasoning powers; the heart and lungs the home of the artistic, for which feeling is needed; and the limbs and metabolism facilitate our dealing with the earthly and by extension to the moral, that through which we engage with the rest of the world. Using the hands and feet for creative skills or crafts trains us in this, for we are dealing with and evaluating the materials of the world and their goodness or otherwise and making our guided impressions upon them.

That is what we can learn with the tiniest variation in the edge of a leaf. The impact/impression/pure experience gives us the mental-picture of, for example, toothedness, pointedness and so on; also heartshapedness, spearshapedness, roundness and so on. It is a much deeper sensation than the mere head knowledge. In plant books there are pages of the different classified leaf shapes; now in our breast region there are their corresponding mental-pictures, each with its gesture, which is felt there as a *sensation* as well as being *known in the mind*. When these are then linked through a metamorphosis, the whole breath of the plant-melody replicates itself *within* us. The resultant mental-picture is alive: we can take up a piece of chalk and let this picture flow down our arm, through the fingers holding the chalk, through the chalk itself that has become part of us and on to the blackboard, without thinking about what we are doing. It may be something like the Zen 'it' that performs these actions of enlightenment, only it becomes possible through mental effort, not meditation or physical exercising. We do not ascribe it to a numinous 'it' but to our *own unique self,* the ego.

Once we have had the tiniest glimpse of this we can understand that there can be a 'concept' of plant, woven together of all these mental-pictures, in space and time, that has power to *create*. Our own live thought can cause a picture of a plant to appear on the board: so may the plant 'type' bring about a real plant for us to look upon.

We can intuit that there is an entity in Nature, unseen to earthly eyes but perceptible to enhanced artistic imagination, that actually works *in* the organs of the plant world, guiding the forms as the material cells divide. What is ascribed alone to genetics is now perceived in its totality. What was thought to be the *cause* of the living organism is grasped now more widely as the projection into the sense world of something that has its reality in an adjacent world. We are on the way to perceiving the Type, which creates in the process of growth, decay and reproduction—a living participation rather than the working of Natural Law in the inanimate world of crystal growth, motion and impact, erosion and so on. These work universally, from outside the phenomenon. It is a signature of the mineral kingdom that form is caused by the material composing it. The signature of the animal kingdom is that form, motion and gesture are the effect of the soul nature of the species, and that of man that we define our own being and destiny (more or less!).

For *knowledge* of the plant kingdom we need to discover the Type, an entity that is alive and expands into life the forms that it builds out of the material offered it, making each 'specimen' unique. Then we can inwardly 'see' the type while outwardly beholding what is before our eyes.

Life itself escapes the confines of equations, rather as does Art. Art can see into the world whose reality is beyond but whose manifestation is here.

7

THE TWELVE SENSES AND THE SPECIAL CASE OF THOUGHT

In Chapter 4, 'What am I seeing when I look?', an inherent sense of *movement* was acknowledged alongside that of sight, to trace the outlines of the different areas of colour that are the essence of the sense of sight. In the next step of identifying what we see, thinking came into play, linking up the respective content of these two senses. To the usually accepted five, a sixth was added. (The 'sixth sense' we sometimes refer to is more an intuitive combination of a complex of sense-perceptible content rather than a pure sense, from which all thought content can be withdrawn.) Further consideration requires others to be added, as the following exploration indicates, even though it is often hard to find a physical foundation for them.

Start with hearing. The larynx produces both sound and word, thereby being a partner to the ear; but to produce words, that extra effort is required that we wrestled with in a forgotten childhood. As adults we may hear someone speaking but be unable to make out what is being said. We then experience the sense of Word struggling to perceive; and it is this sense that has awakened into action as we learned to speak. In another experience, it may be that we hear the words clearly but cannot make sense of them. Here it is a sense for Thought that makes itself felt. The brain is widely considered as the *producer* of thoughts but practising the leaf exercises can demonstrate that although some thoughts can be produced fairly randomly by the brain (especially when we are trying to concentrate on one thought) we are able to make others through our conscious artistic ability. These the brain then perceives; and our thinking observes the relationships that then manifest within what is perceived. Now we have eight senses.

Carrying this still one stage further one can detect in the meaning and the way it is expressed something of the character of the person speaking (*per-son*, from the Latin for something *sounding through*). There is a sense for the physical presence of a real being there, essentially invisible to eye or ear, yet perceptible. One has come to the sense of ego. This is a physical sense that perceives the projection into the sense-world of the true spiritual being of someone else. Now we have nine senses.

To see whether these are in fact physical senses it helps to cast an eye over the scheme Rudolf Steiner gradually built up through his work. He places their initial formation at the very beginning of evolution as aspects of the original *physical* body (an entity composed purely of warmth) before it had life, their rudiments being impressed by the twelve directional forces of the periphery, the antecedents of what are now the constellations of the Zodiac. Considering that the first rudiment of the earthly body of both man and the earth was of warmth (referred to already as an element in its own right rather than a property of matter), the *sense* of warmth would be considered the primal one. In Steiner's sequence we can descend from there through sight, smell and taste (see later), then to the more bodily senses of touch, life, movement and balance; or we can ascend to the more spiritual ones of hearing, word, thought and ego. In this way there are twelve. Thinking is, as we have seen, the faculty of perceiving the relationships between these, including the perceptions of the sense of Thought. It is this attribute of the human being, an extension of our self-awareness, that Steiner regards as the real separator between the human and animal kingdoms, the real hallmark of our humanity in its inner life. We met another aspect of this in the last chapter as the ability to rise beyond Nature.

Our exercises are *based* on making thought pictures of something that we have perceived with our senses. We are then moving from the sense of sight—or the content of *any* sense perception—to that of *thought and the non-physical activity of thinking*. Our *sense* of thought (perceiving thoughts) and our *activity* of thought (letting thoughts combine harmoniously with each other) bring different images of the sense-world into relationship and movement and hence *meaning*.

In Steiner's conception of the human being, the physical body—the part that is sense-*perceptible*—is fundamentally also a sense-*perceiver*. The other parts of the physical body are related to and influenced by parts evolved later. Man's becoming upright frees these senses from the earthly domain and he becomes the one *who looks up*; Greek '*anthropos*' (as in Anthropology—or Anthroposophy). He places his body in the upright position where he is crowned by the circle of the zodiac with its twelve constellations or 'stars'; so there are twelve *bodily* senses within this scheme. Schemes are a way of forcing something alive and fluid into a thinkable form hence they always lose something in transition; so if one thinks, 'Ah, but . . .' one might very well be on the right path from the *scheme* to the *living reality*.

The twelve senses readily group themselves into three groups of four, although other groupings are also possible, as with the zodiac itself. The upper four have been touched on already: ego, thought, word, hearing. The first three are the more spiritual of the bodily senses. At the other or lower end are touch, life, movement and balance. The last three are clearly more deeply set within the organism and are often not thought of as senses at all; but you only have to lose your balance or feel 'one degree under' to access the relevant senses and recognize them as such. It's fun to shut your eyes when the train you are in is about to leave the station and see if you can 'sense' when the motion begins, ('seeing' with your eyes shut).

In between these two groups is a third, including four of the five familiar senses: warmth, sight, taste and smell. They progress through the elements: fire, air, water and earth respectively, for the sense of smell actually senses the fine particles that an object releases.

The key point here is that each of these senses can themselves be the subject of our observation exercises and can be developed to become the heralds, through Form, Metamorphosis and Gesture, of a world that informs that of matter. It is *form* through which a complex existing being finally becomes accessible to our senses. That therefore is the starting point—twelve of them—of our journeying back to the source: a world that has its *being* beyond these senses yet reaches into our world of freedom through these twelve windows. Poetically, and perhaps not only so, the link between these twelve soul windows and the twelve stars crowning our upright posture tells of the relationship between our two realms of existence: earthly life and that before and after. Can we access that through moving from Word to Thought to Being to enter into a communion of knowledge with a world we previously only saw? What *can* you see? Then, 'What can you *know*?'

8

GLIMPSING THE ETHER

If we look at a river flowing over rocks, we see the waves created by their interplay apparently streaming *back upstream*. What we need to do now is to soften our gaze to a more peripheral awareness rather than a sharp central looking. This peripheral seeing is what we do most of the time unless something catches our attention or we are searching for something. We do this while walking along without especially concentrating on anything in particular, taking in *everything* until something awakens us and we bring our focussed gaze to bear upon it. We need now to learn to return to the wider mode without losing our watchful eye for detail. This can feel as though we are perceiving from a large dish behind our head instead of from a point between our eyes. We have practised very much the focussed looking when studying forms, then the more open one for metamorphosis, using the peripheral gaze to bring all that we have observed into a single picture that reaches into our soul more deeply. One may feel that these two modes of perception are somewhat male and female; the male mode too often having dominated the science of the previous two centuries, linked as it is to an intellect emancipating itself from an older wisdom. In recent times, one sees how the female, peripheral, soul mode may gradually be changing that. Now back to the river: as the volume and speed of flow fluctuates, these waves appear to be straining free from the rock to flow against the water itself. Our eyes see the flow of water downstream but another sense perceives the flow of form upstream. This perception is the result of the interplay of these senses of sight, movement and thought and takes us to the edge of physical sense perception. Of course, this impression fades away when we focus directly on the movement of the water; movement that can be explained scientifically and expressed in mathematical formulae. Nevertheless, the experience we can have of the water flowing upstream is a repeatable phenomenon that adds something of value and interest to an imaginative observer who takes this peripheral approach. Here is an example of the 'organ' of our whole being adding something valid to the science of experience without contradicting traditional scientific laws. It should also be noted that a peripheral approach to observation in no way implies a relaxing of the visual faculties. On the contrary, greater effort must be summoned to sharpen one's awareness of the periphery of sight and equally of all sense impression.

Another example of what we can experience with peripheral observation is this: when a fire is burning in the grate, tongues of flame reach upwards; but between them round, dark forms are to be seen, that, as the flames strive upwards, appear to be striving downwards into them. 'Something' flows counter to the visible flow.

These are two examples of the threshold of the sense-world where forces counter to the physical forces can be seen to manifest. Steiner refers to this 'counter'-space as the etheric world. By developing, strengthening and applying this peripheral awareness in plant observation, its leaves, petals and so on, we become sensitive to what is working formatively through the spaces *between* the organs or *in* the curvature of a particular organ. A very modest gazing can sense, for example, whether these forces are weak or strong, vital or not, and further observational work over centuries or by particularly gifted people has perceived qualities in these forces that can be used for healing and other applications. We need, however, to bear in mind that peripheral *seeing* is not the same as peripheral *awareness*. The first is needed in the two above examples; the second whenever we go from mental detail to the complete mental-picture. In both cases the central seeing is that of detail and is close to the intellect whereas peripheral seeing takes in the whole and then moves to the detail. Thinking of these as male and female modes immediately reveals that both need to be mastered and integrated for seeing anything completely.

It is in between these two worlds, the senses and the mind, that thinking dwells, where the world of matter refines over into one of *life*. As we have already noted, the faculty of thought has two sides: *perceiving* thoughts or the quality of someone else's thought and *creating* new thoughts. But even good thinking exists in the material world; it does not live. The plant picture we created does not grow and blossom, except in our imagination. Further practice of the right kind of exercises described for example in Anthroposophy does, however, result in freeing thinking from the material of the brain, releasing it into the realm of the living. There it does have an effect on the surroundings. Creating thought as mentioned above is really the effort of sorting our thoughts to connect together and monitoring that process, discarding what does not belong. We 'see' when it is right, for a new and greater thought *appears*, just as light *appears* when matter is brought into the right state of excitation (see below). This is where thinking is so important in the context of spiritual study and productivity, for it is the lowest rung on the ladder of the spirit. *Feeling* remains too closely connected to our own inner world for this to be as free but feeling is *essential* in bringing the thoughts to life and clothing them in humanity.

★ ★ ★

In our work of training our seeing we are closely connected to the element of *light*. Light makes itself the parable for all perception but, like the eye, cannot be perceived when we are seeing. Light too plays at a kind of frontier between the earthly world and a finer one, captured by the term ether-light or even light-ether, as one of the kinds of ether (like those related to water and heat described above). Anthroposophy contains a vast amount of material on the theme, both in Steiner and in his students, for further study.

A point of entry into this world of glimpsing the ether, therefore, is to *observe* light. How can we observe something that is not visible, or, how can we come to see that light *is* invisible? Here are two exercises to help with this. First, when the sun is out, stand facing away from it and look at the landscape or scenery, noticing all the qualities of light and shadow, their relative strength and contrast. Then turn around and do the same looking in the direction of the sun. How does the contrast of light and shadow appear then? Turn to the left and to the right and do the same there, in this case with the sun coming from either side. In each direction, the whole quality of the view is different: we are looking into the workshop of light and shade together.

After studying the light-shade matrix in these four sun-related directions, move on to the following. Look at the blue sky (again in the same four directions). What is the *quality* of the blue? Is it clear and deep, or hazy? Is it radiating light or absorbing it? Then look at the clouds in each direction. Are they radiating the light or rather absorbing it? Do they dazzle, shade or have a silver lining? Next, with shielded eyes, look in the direction of the sun. What degree of warmth can we feel? Is it a dazzling or a gentle light? (This varies considerably through day and year.) Finally look at tree trunks or, if possible, bare earth, say a newly ploughed field or a face of freshly split rock. How does the light reflect from them? How do they give it back to us?

After gaining some familiarity with these exercises, a clear difference in each direction and each light source is discerned. However, one must not over-simplify and lose detail: summer woodland light reflected from leaves has its own quality of radiance. Note the difference between the reflected light off holly (which has quite a strong sharp gleam, almost a glitter), ivy (a softer shine, even though still very bright) and bramble leaves, which though bright, give a still softer sheen. Other leaves just remain neutral, softly being themselves. There are many ways of describing the qualities of the light reflected thus. In each case the 'reflected' light has a different quality from clouds or sky, yet also different from bare ground or tree-trunks. There will gradually be sensed the qualities of earth, water, air and fire: the fieriness of the sun, the wateriness of clouds, the airiness of the blue sky and the earthiness of the bare ground. These four elemental qualities each signal one of four etheric forces—the tools of the beings described in Chapter 4. They are usually termed warmth ether, light ether, chemical or tone ether (since it governs harmony, both of sounds and of chemical combination) and life ether.

Where is light? Everything we see, we do so because of its relationship to light, the way it gives it back after receiving it in its own special way. But where is light originally? We are taught about the 'velocity' of light as though it were analogous to sound; yet the sense of sight is more analogous to our sense of thinking than hearing—'I see', also meaning 'I understand'. Illumination as understanding, arrived at through the activity of our ego, shines upon the words we see, hear, or feel, to bring their meaning into focus. In this, our ego really can be experienced as the light of our world—and relates to 'the light of the world' (John: 8, 12). Seeing, related as it must be to light, is less able to penetrate into the depth of things than hearing. Through hearing, the 'deep cause' of a body's particular light-giving nature is to be found, when we start to perceive the quality of its inner toning. We saw above how hearing leads to word then through thought (already something 'light') to ego. When we see the light in someone's eyes, which is always a near-transcendent sensation, we are closer to their soul and sometimes their ego too. This, *our* 'ego light', enables us to perceive more deeply into the essence of others. It is *our* light—and it has no velocity! Using the idea of man as microcosm, this ego light can be seen as an image of the *macrocosmic* light—*that also has no velocity*—bestowing 'ego light' upon the world in a completely non-egotistical way. *I* am the light of the world. Outer light reveals to us spatial relationships whilst ego light reveals spiritual relationships between people, and indeed to the spiritual world as we found by moving from sense observation through thinking to Being.

We met in Chapter 1 the Plant Being of elementary 'duration' that was, however, an image of the slightly higher plant *spirit* having greater duration; and in turn we saw perhaps how modest things of the sense world, that grow, move or change with time, relate to archetypes of cosmic dimension and aeonal duration. So too with light. For example, when we gaze at the stars, we see a light of cosmic dimension that is experienced as existing without duration or velocity if perceived with 'ego light' or 'peripheral awareness'. In this, the totality of experience is imbued with quality and qualitative relationships that impart a true and meaningful aspect of reality that is not reducible to photons and velocities, but has a spiritual validity which we can all grasp, if we allow ourselves to do so. It felt wrong to be told as a child that the stars we see are not there anymore. The child knows that that is not true until this knowledge is 'educated' out ('*in*ducation', indoctrination); then it becomes really difficult to loosen oneself from this idea of velocity. People think you are mad or from another planet (or a star that no longer exists). What can we do? How can we think about this? The 'velocity of light' is the 'velocity' of phenomena *connected with* light taking place within the realm of *matter*. As such, it founds a science capable of exploring the cosmos physically, materially. *Beyond* matter, light is Being and as such has no velocity.

There is no quick solution but here are two further thoughts that might help. First, for us as sensory beings, light is never perceived directly, only given back from objects, but it does connect objects together in our field of vision. No single light 'source' is really the origin of light. The apparent source may be a wire, or gas, excited matter that then *radiates*. Matter cannot create light but it can and does *reveal* light. True light is more *directly* revealed to us as an experience at the moment of perception, through thought and ego. In this moment, we can realise ourselves as light-bearers, bearing the light within our experience and thus related by light to the ultimate light-bearer of the cosmos, reuniting us as microcosm to the macrocosmic world. Secondly, even the modern conception that the sun's light is an emission from nuclear reactions only presents the *material* conditions for light to appear. When we think, we sometimes say, 'It appears to me . . .', implying that there is another dimension that will manifest in our thinking when the conditions there are right. Within the sun, according to the mathematical models, matter, in order to reach the state where it can emit light, has to undergo immense pressure and transformation; the faithful atoms and molecules of our sense world have to be rendered down to a state of pure heat before the light process can begin. So too, in ourselves, we may experience immense pressure and transformation when crossing inner thresholds towards new insight and understanding. On a smaller scale, we can also remember the thresholds marking the transitions from hearing to word, to thought and to being, and can see that each transition illuminates a deeper aspect of Being. We can say that light, when observed and considered qualitatively, takes on the mantle of Being: a sun being, a constellation being or more. Into this being or these beings I can enter with my *own* being; into the concept of sun atoms fusing together I can enter with my thoughts—but not my being! My ego simply refuses to go there; therefore there is no true *light* there. Just reflect on the difference of feeling between externally given knowledge and that worked out on the basis of one's own experience. Our methods distinguish between reality and provisional hypotheses. They guard that the latter are not then assumed to be real but encourage us to take them as stimulus for further true perceptions.

We can now move further from what we have *seen* in the ways described above into the realms of sound, word, thought and being. There is much to hear in Nature but when light plays in, imagination awakes and hearing may give birth to word—understanding—and ultimately to being. This is examined in some more depth later, where these methods are applied to observation of rocks. In the meantime, it is a wonderfully fruitful exercise to take a new revelation and render it into word, from where it can be heard by others, and seen.

★   ★   ★

Recalling the system of sense organs from the previous chapter we rise from seeing, which can stand for all the senses, to warmth. This leads in Nature to the finer phenomena of light, tone and life. In ourselves seeing leads through warmth of engagement to hearing and word: the creative word of life. From there we move up to meaning or thought, then to being or ego. The way of observing and thinking opens into perception of being, where our ego, which resides with us on the earth, meets the ego of the plant (and other entities of Nature) in its home in worlds higher than the earthly. This does not yet mean true spiritual perception but as it were a projection of it from higher realms into our earthly one. This is at once a preview in feeling of what such knowledge might be like.

9

BARE TREES IN JANUARY

The New Year wind roars out its presence without any resistance from leaves on the trees, for these are bare. The wind tunes itself to their forking shapes and we hear the woodland symphony.

The January sun, too, plays on the trees. We see the branching tips and perhaps recognize the tree species accordingly; but there is now colour too, emerging out of a Winter sleep; for both the new twig growth and the buds it bears move from winter grey into colour. These are the colours of the youngest bark and of the bud scales. There is the gentle grey of the ash with its bold black buds; there is the warm indigo of the thin birch twigs with their slate-mauve buds; and strikingly too there shines out the golden orange of new willow.

The light often has a golden hue at this time of the year, sending the cloud colour to gentle purple. The interplay between all these highlights different parts of the distant woods in gently flowing colour.

Here, then, we have the *forms* of branches, including their colours, brought into spatial movement to combine to a very archetypal picture of January. As the months progress, this picture undergoes change, each month with its own gesture. The bud colours give way to various greens, hiding the twigs. You might feel that within the overall green there are nuances of every other colour, each experiencing itself as green. Later, the fresh green becomes darker green and less differentiated, until in June new growth appears here and there to pepper the old green with a lighter tone, or even a reddish hue. By now the predations of insect life affect the leaves but in the following weeks the time of gold comes and soon the leaves fly, each in its own movement, until only the evergreens are left. Here is another kind of metamorphosis, a metamorphosis of gestures, that lets us build for ourselves a gesture of gestures: that of the whole year.

Rudolf Steiner created a building to be a house for his work and introduced into the architecture the use of different timbers for the columns that supported the roof. This building was to make manifest to us the laws and processes lying behind the sense world. One of these is the influence of each planet, another the principle of their metamorphosis. He had named the great epochs of evolution with the names we now use for the planets and he carved the columns to portray these characteristics.

The seven make up a metamorphosis that reveals the forces behind evolution: seven long stages of development interwoven with non-perceptible periods of assimilation and preparation. These changes are much greater than we have so far seen in plant development and are shown artistically by the inherent gesture of each carving.

To be more precise, these 'planets' are spheres around Earth and around or within the Sun sphere. Each sphere is inside the next larger one. The visible planet is, so to speak, a material deposit where radial and peripheral forces are nearly in balance, like a milestone where the influence of that planet ends. The spheres also breathe (according to the constellation of Sun, Planet and Earth) in and out, due to the eccentricity of their apparent orbits. In the modern conception of the Solar System, the Sun plays a central role as all the planets appear to orbit it in ellipses. To pursue the relativity of this further, look in Rudolf Steiner's course, GA 323, 'Third Scientific Course, Astronomy'. It is difficult terrain but very fruitful.

Obviously other models arise when the standpoint changes, in particular the view from the Earth. Because the Earth orbits the Sun, the planets' orbits taken around the Earth are not ellipses but curves called epicycles. The curves make loops according to whether the planet is at its nearest or farthest. By analogy with Chapter 3 where we tried to imagine the 'sun-sphere' as the surface created by an elliptical hoop spun on its rim, a planetary sphere will vary in size between those spheres mapped out at the nearest and farthest points of the orbit.

It may be puzzling to think of 'spheres' here when the planets lie on a flat plane through the Earth. But when the spiritual forces that place a planet where it is are investigated we discover one set of forces radiating out from the sun and another raying in from the depths of space (these will one day slow down the expansion of the universe). These obviously radiate outwards and inwards spherically. They balance each other where the planet is but with a small place of imbalance that allows some of the substance of that planet's sphere to materialise. What we know as the planet is just the overlap of a tiny part of the causative spheres. Anyway, the rotation of the planet is related to the behaviour of these spheres and the result for us on the Earth, together with its plant life, is that the spheres surround us, are sometimes near and sometimes farther away. At these points they are fairly stable but in between the expansion or contraction of the sphere is stronger and therefore stronger in its effect on the Earth.

Considering all the planets as well as the sun and moon, it is clear that the heavenly spheres have a very complex and never repeating movement. We have mentioned heavenly beings as having to do with the planets, Spirits of Form, Movement and Wisdom. The movement of these planetary spheres is thus an embodiment of their activities. The Earth is thus embraced by a series of living sheathes that revolve and pulsate in a way that has a certain periodicity in its parts but where there is no repetition in the whole. And we and the rest of Nature live in the centre of these influences, in perpetual evolution.

Acquiring a sense for the different planetary gestures allows one to perceive their different influences upon the plant, or other aspect of creation (whether natural or human). For example, the elm leaf has a marked asymmetry where the blade arises out of the stalk, and tight curves reminiscent of the tight curves made by its planet Mercury as seen in the sky. The same curve is seen in other trees, like the hazel. So this feature of the leaf has a Mercury archetype. However the *flower* of the hazel is more like that of the birch (Venus) and the fruit more like that of the oak (Mars).

As in evolution there are smaller cycles within larger ones, so the plant world is arranged in planetary hierarchies. The seven used by Steiner for the building were:

Hornbeam—Saturn; Maple—Jupiter; Oak—Mars; Ash—Sun; Elm—Mercury; Birch—Venus; Cherry—Moon.

However, these archetypal trees are all *deciduous* and form but one of seven similar groups within the plant kingdom. The deciduous trees are governed by Jupiter, majestic and strong. Other groups are Saturn, conifers; Mars, shrubs; Sun, herbs; Mercury, climbing plants; Venus, alpine plants; Moon, cacti and succulents. Frits Julius has developed this thoroughly in his book, *Metamorphosis* and also related these seven to stages of human life and character.

What about different types of conifer or of shrubs etc.? There are tree-like shrubs (Jupiter within the Mars group) like the elder and shrub-like trees (Mars within the Jupiter group), the apple for instance, with its impetuous outreaching shoots that become the base for further growth. And within conifers there is the elegant larch with its bright flowers (Venus) or the great cedars (Jupiter) or the regularly branched redwoods (Saturn). Thus within each of these seven may be found again seven sub-types and in the other direction, overarching all, seven great kingdoms. Four of these are currently manifest in Nature, with Man being the pivotal link between Nature and Spirit, out of which a further three will arise in future cycles of evolution, as transformations of the lower three through the creative co-operation of mankind with the beings and forces of the spirit. Imagine a family tree where each sibling has its own seven offspring and at the top is the unifying principle of creation itself.

Let us now look at some of these branches in detail.

A branch of any of the above will appear as a confusion of twiggery with angles and bumps everywhere, so start by looking at the outside tip. Things are simpler here, for each tree finishes its complex growth with a length of simple growth, which we can define as a 'growth unit'. By starting at the very tip of the outermost twig there are seen to be one or more buds, depending on the species. Following the twig back down the stem away from this bud, other buds are to be seen, at various positions around it and with varying intervals between them. At a certain point there is a change in the smoothness and colour of the stem and probably a concentration of side stems or the remnants of old buds. These signs show that the stem further back is older. Go back another stretch and a second, similar, transition is to be found. The whole branch can then be ordered into younger and older growth units. Now by looking at the outermost two units it can be seen on examination that they have the same basic pattern, the difference being that where on the youngest (outermost) stretch of stem there are buds, on the next older there are no buds as such but side growth. These have grown from the buds of the last growth season. We gain the insight that from a bud there grows not a single leaf as might be assumed but a *stem with several leaves*. This point is often very difficult for students to grasp or accept. Try at this point to imagine away all these newer growths, pop them back into their buds, and there, in imagination, is the branch as it was last season—then the season before that, and so on. Last year, the year before—sometimes there is more than one growth spell within one year—we are moving back in time. But we can also go the other way and run the picture forwards, giving a sense of the growth *pulse* that creates a tree. We let each of the buds on the newest growth unit open and grow. How will they grow? This pulse is probably best seen in a wild cherry of about ten to fifteen years old. The trunk is straight and most of the branches grow outwards in groups of five from the same point, then another burst a few feet further up, all clean and rhythmic. The past is to be seen right before our eyes and the future too, in invisible picture. In some trees *most* of the buds grow new stems (birch), in others only a few do (oak). Sometimes the longer side stems are in the *middle* of the older stem (hornbeam), sometimes at the base or even at the top (elm). Sometimes some of the growth has *died off* (birch and oak), sometimes buds have not opened. The variety is endless, the scheme below (p. 60) showing the planetary variations. But now, in the present, there stands before us a perception of the waves of growth that have *actually happened* and it is clear from observation what the *typical* behaviour of the species is.

Has there been a flower? If so, it is seen that growth ends there. Where this appears not to be so, closer observation finds a very small stem bearing flowers along it just as the typical growth unit bore leaves. Maple is the archetype for this. We found in the previous discussion of Metamorphosis (Chapter 3) that metamorphosis of *side*-growth is further advanced towards its goal, the blossom. The more side-growth there is, as is the case with trees, the more do *blossoms* appear instead of leaves. That indeed is what gives a tree its natural size: all the growth becomes blossom; but cut a branch off and soon more leaf growth will appear. Cut in the wrong place and the tree form is thrown out of balance, as can be seen where gales have removed branches. Pruning is best done out of knowledge of the growth unit and its metamorphosis in time.

Going back to the growth unit, it was remarked that its buds were set at varying intervals. There is a slight thickening of the stem at each bud, called a *node*. The stem between buds is called the internode. It is usually short at the bottom of the growth, lengthens in the middle and later decreases. Where, as in the oak or ash, there is a cluster of buds at the tip, these can be seen to be, as it were, a compression of the same growth pattern out of the spiral into a plane. As with annuals, with their blossom at the top of the stem, one can sense that plants as they grow are met with invisible forces that contain their growth. This is most obviously seen in the flowering impulse. Materially, it is from below up but from the aspect of *form* it is from above down, as will shortly be seen in the way the buds are set on the stem (nutation). Some familiarity with the exercises of the earlier chapters paves the way to grasping this invisible 'force from outside'.

The full growth unit is therefore divided up into these internodes between consecutive buds. Look closer to see that beneath each bud is a little scar or 'cicatrice' that observation at other seasons reveals to be where a leaf has dropped. Moving up the stem, therefore, there is a fourfold *process* that *repeats*: stem—node—leaf—bud. Opening of the buds in Spring soon shows that each produces its own whole *stem* (see above), rather than a single leaf, and this fourfold process repeats itself. This is to be added to our concept of the threefold leaf (base, stalk, surface) and is a valuable tool of observation when unravelling the occasional complexities of growth, enabling one to decipher the 'confusion of twiggery' that a large tree may present. Every tiny feature on the whole tree is explicable by these two features, the three and the four.

It helps us grasp how the majesty of great trees (the Jupiter trees) and their complex but species-typical branching style is accounted for in the simple rules the growth unit receives from its parent planet(s), influenced then by the two factors that work in a direction opposite to growth: blossoming and dieback. There is our tree, between growth and flowering or death. By examining the trees that Steiner selected to represent the planetary archetypes it is found that all the possible variations of growth and branching are represented (see scheme on p. 60).

These archetypal trees present images in plant growth of the curving, spiralling paths of the planets as seen from the earth. They are most noticeable in the placing of the buds on a stem. The strange thing is that it does not matter where the planet is in the sky, its influence works universally, as though the outer planet were but a kind of marker (see above) of a particular celestial force that sends its influences upon the living things of the earth as though in spirals. (See 'vertical' and 'spiral tendency' in Chapter 3.) If you are familiar with the outer, naked eye, movements of these planets, this 'idea' will feel more realistic, for you will know the feeling of the quick gestures of Mercury in contrast to the steady looping of Saturn and Jupiter. Karl Mier developed this in this country. He had attended Rudolf Steiner's extraordinary course on agriculture held on the Koberwitz estate near Breslau in 1924 (one of his last). He went on to teach naked eye observation of the heavens with a view to helping farmers bring these planetary mysteries into their own living observation of the life in their charge. His methods are well expanded and recorded in Norman Davidson's book, *Sky Phenomena* (Lindisfarne Books 2004).

When these spiral forces encounter the upsurging vitality of the plant, the interplay is, so to speak, registered in the cambium below the bark (before its formation, of course) and a node develops as mentioned above in the 'growth unit'. The individual trees make visible this interplay between cosmic forces and earthly ones and specifically according to planetary type. (Ernst Michael Kranich, *Planetary Influences on Plants*, Floris Books; Frits Julius, *Metamorphose*, Mellinger Verlag 1969, translation in preparation.) Here is an instance where these forces are manifest before our eye.

Not only are these spirals to be found in the nutation. There is also a variety of spirals visible in the centres of composite flowers and indeed already in the outlines of the scales of the buds before they open. The pioneer researcher of these, Lawrence Edwards (*The Field of Form*, Floris

Books 1982) found exact geometry for them and, moreover, correlations between subtle changes in their forms and certain constellations of their respective planets. This is one example of these connections that really comes down into earthly demonstrable fact. Lawrence Edwards held workshops in projective geometry that gave people the chance to see mentally the mostly two-dimensional spaces that the growth of plants and other natural phenomena generate within our every-day three-dimensional one. This was for me another valuable tool for seeing the world in a more flexible way than one had been educated to do and such courses are recommended as invaluable aids to transforming one's gaze. One caution, however: the geometry of plant growth needs ever to ask what this or that constant or variable in the mathematics *actually means* in the world of Nature forces and Nature spirits.

As Winter returns, many of these trees will again be bare; and later still, some of them will have become firewood. In the grate, the flames are a beautiful mystery, yet they have their typical forms and colours. This mystery is naturally veiled unless the fire is of a single species of wood only. Each species of tree has its own flame! Colour, form, temperament, spark!

Later still, each ash too has its own qualities, treasured by potters to glaze their ware. Some of this ware may be vases into which new bare twigs can be placed in January to enjoy, to observe!

To use this chart, first note the planetary symbols at the side, arranged from outer to inner planets: Saturn, Jupiter, Mars, Sun, Venus, Mercury and Moon. On the seven-point star above them they are arranged so that this sequence is found in alternate positions going anticlockwise, whereas a clockwise direction gives their evolutionary sequence and at the same time that of the days of the week. That is their dynamic, which brings movement (metamorphosis) down into the realm of life on Earth.

Below each leaf are the three attributes of the lamina or blade: simple or compound/form/margin. A few of their variations are mentioned in Chapter 2 but many more are to be found in botanical works. The first column to the right describes the arrangement of the buds on the growth unit or basic stem. All possibilities are present within the seven. Next is shown the degree to which these buds actually bring forth branches. 'Onward Growth' is the widely varying ways exhibited by these trees whereas Die-Back shows a near symmetry between far and near, with the sun in the centre.

Within flower and fruit again there is great variety and it becomes clear that this sevenfoldness covers nearly all varieties of the forms and

Planetary Trees Compared

Planetary Trees Compared

	Nutation	Branching
♄ Hornbeam *carpinus betulus* simple/lanceolate/serrate	alternating	very regular
♃ Maple *acer pseudo-platanus* compound/palmate/entire	opposed, crossed	irregular
♂ Oak *quercus robur* simple/obovate/sinuate, lobed	spiral, 5 buds at tip	very irregular
☉ Ash *fraxinus excelsior* compound/pinnate/serrate	opposed, crossed	regular below irregular above
♀ Birch *betula pendula* simple/rhomboid or triangular/double serrate	spiral, single bud at tip	very regular
☿ Elm *ulmus glabra* simple/lanceolate, oval or cordate/serrate; then obovate/doubly serrate	alternate	very regular
☽ cherry *prunus padus* simple/lanceolate/serrate	spiral, 5 buds at tip	regular, 5 branches per year

	Onward growth	Die-back from axils or branches	Blossoms male	female	Fruit	Summer growth?
♄	via all axils	little	catkins before leaves on tips of last yrs growth	chains from axils		yes
♃	first at the tips then by forking	much at tips little at sides	combined at the tips			no
♂	at and near the tips	very much	catkins both growing from axils during leaf growth	simple blossoms		yes
☉	strong centre at the tip but later to the sides without a centre. weaker lower down the stem	moderate	many bunched on the stalk: before leaves open	: during : leaf growth : from their · axils		no
♀	through all axil buds	very much	catkins from last year at end of twig	catkins on short stalks during leaf growth		yes
☿	through top three buds	little at top of stem, much below	petalless blossoms before leaves, on two year old growth			yes
☽	main stem and its five top buds; irregular on side branches	moderate	rosettes of 5 blossoms around twig tip, before leaves emerge from the centre bud there			no

occurrence to be found throughout this world of deciduous trees. By learning to recognise them all on their home tree one can begin to recognise the same features as one notices them on a different tree. The author, when given a demonstration of this long ago, was fascinated as though by a conjuring trick, but extremely sceptical. Later it does become more obvious. The thesis simply is that as the planetary spheres interpenetrate (see above) they are extremely mobile (coming as they do under the aegis of Spirits of Motion referred to in Chapter 5). This can be a free thesis—one can discover it as one becomes more familiar with Gesture.

To conclude, here is a further development of the two examples given above, hazel and apple. There is another common tree like the hazel but preferring wetter ground, the alder. It has catkins not unlike those of the hazel, forming in the same way, but the fruits are very different. While the hazel nuts were likened to the oak apple the alder bears cones, which link it to Saturn and the conifers. This Saturn influence (duration) also shows in these cones staying on the branch a good year or more. Then, the leaves are similar but with important differences: the hazel has its broad point in the middle or towards the base whereas the alder's is towards the tip, creating an outgoing gesture, like the oak yet without its undulations. It also lacks the mercurial curve at the base and the strong asymmetry of the elm. Both trees are traditionally connected to the realms of faery and magic.

The apple is a wonderful tree. We compared it to a shrub, bringing in the branches a Mars gesture on to the Jupiter quality of the trunk (the sign of a 'real' tree). This shrub gesture is primarily in the long outward and downward curvature of the branches. They begin with the upward striving of their parental Jupiter nature but as they lengthen they curve downwards under their own weight, since they are no longer held in uprightness by Jupiter, Sun or Saturn. They come then more under the influence of Venus to blossom and Mars to bear fruit, the latter increasing the curvature with sheer weight. The best example of this shrub curvature is the Elder. It reveals a wonderful two-year cycle of long shoots one year that are weighed down by berries round and black and full of Sun power after a fragrant show of Venus influence in the blossoms. What was at first upright is now the curve of Mars and Frits Julius' arm. Some people use the flowers of elder as a tea to bring out a fever. One can imagine the tiny blossoms with their huge supply of pollen bringing sunshine into the sufferer to purge the causes of the fever, harmonising its burning, purging process and leading it over to healthy human aery warmth.

Carrying this image of the shrub's curve, we see the apple as enjoying it to the full, within its treeness, introducing into it the two-year fruiting-branch process that belongs to the shrubs—one year growth, next year flowers and fruit. Woe betide the gardener who ignores this when pruning!

10

THE PLANT'S PLACE WITHIN THE FOUR
KINGDOMS OF NATURE

Now, after entering into the movements that play such an essential role in giving a plant its form, imagine in place of the plant a simple crystal. It too has form but one completely unlike that of the plant. There are no movements. See how the faces and edges are arranged in three-dimensional but parallel perspective, with opposing pairs meeting in the infinitely distant—creative fantasy could say, amongst the stars. This fantasy can *see* the qualitative difference between this stable, eternal, mineral form and the developing, spiralling forms and metamorphoses of the plant. One might perceive through this ordered feeling the essential difference between star forces and planetary forces and be able to say, 'The plant too has a mineral body but the forms associated with the mineral kingdom are, in the plant, completely displaced by those of the realm of life.' The plant is a planetary being whilst the mineral's home is in the stars.

The Plant as a Kingdom, high in fluid content, has been released from the rigid structures of the mineral world to be shaped by the rhythmic forces of the circling planets. The life-sustaining liquid movement and circulation of saps therefore distinguishes the Plant Kingdom from the Mineral Kingdom as water is distinguishable from earth. One has the impression that the Plant Kingdom has lost the immortality of the mineral world, but has received instead a capacity for change and diverse growth, albeit limited. It can adapt its archetypal form to respond to environmental change, but does not yet really have the freedom to seek out new environments. In the plant, *life* is asserted, and the mineral quality of formation extinguished, overridden by it.

This can then be taken further, to the Animal Kingdom, where the inner metamorphosis of the plant leaf returns as one of vertebrae and skull. Here, movement is no longer anchored in the earth and restricted to the rhythmic cycles of plant growth and decay but has been released, as the animal moves about to explore its environment and even to seek out different landscapes farther afield. This freer movement is the fundamental gesture of animals, although its precursor may also be seen in some of the pollination processes of the plants. The dominant or determining forces that work to give form to animals have displaced the more contained rhythmic elements within plants. Here, the rhythmic forces of plant circulation return in animal circulation and the rhythms of the respiratory system. These are accompanied by the nervous system to create a capacity for sensation and feeling that is absent in plants. To grasp an essential aspect of the Animal Kingdom that is so closely connected to its environment through its refined sense experience, we only have to reflect on our own experience of breathing in when we need to be alert or on guard or breathing out when we are content and at ease. The qualities of sympathy and antipathy, pleasure and pain, and every shade of experience and sensation in between, define this soul realm and prime the nervous system for reproduction, fight or flight and the many other forms of complex free movement that allow this kingdom to survive and flourish. Here both the life rhythm element of the plant and the spatial form element of the mineral are overridden and the *soul* element asserted. Just watch an animal race across a field, a fish leap a waterfall, a bird soar to the sun or an ant crawl its intentional way! Movement is the key to this kingdom and is an expression of *soul*.

Man, humanity? In 'human nature' is not there also to be seen images of this soul realm: lion-hearted, cocky and so on? We can recognize these attributes in ourselves (easier of course in others) and if not change them at least change their effects upon those we encounter. This is the essential potential that places the Human Kingdom in a dual position: part of the rest of Nature yet able to transcend her. Man can *choose* to transform his innate animal qualities and instincts and assert his own morality according to his free, considered judgement; yet, on the other hand, he may equally choose not to take the trouble, or just not even choose at all. We have a much greater capacity for freedom here, but the animal has no choice but to follow its 'nature'. This motif will be developed in the final chapters.

Overview:

Kingdom	Mineral	Plant	Animal	Human
Active State of Matter	Solid	Liquid	Airy	Conceptual
Spatial Influence	Distant Stars	Planets	External Environment	Internal Environment
Species' Life Cycles	Eons	Millennia	Centuries	Decades
Determining Force	Heat and Pressure	Circulation	Instinct	Conscience
Form and Gesture	Linear Geometry	Spiral— Rhythmic	Free Movement	Self-Directed
Freedom or Self-Determination	None	Basic	Moderate	Extensive

So, to summarise the metamorphosis of the determining forces acting on the different kingdoms, we can see that they have different degrees of influence within space and time. The broad brush strokes are laid out here, for simplicity; but we should remain aware that Nature is often at its most interesting when it springs upon us unusual examples showing the transition between these main kingdoms. The most distant stars share their seemingly eternal, unchanging qualities with the stable forms of the Mineral Kingdom. The planets and to a lesser extent the zodiacal constellations of the Sun and Moon are, by contrast, much closer to us; their rhythmic cycles enliven the contained but fluid nature of the Plant Kingdom. The much closer proximity of our immediate environment, our climate, atmosphere and weather system, is defined by the energetic complex movements of the gaseous state of matter and is mirrored in the much freer movement gesture of the Animal Kingdom, the higher animals being distinguished by their breathing and nerve-sense activity. Lastly, Human Beings, when acting according to their higher ideals and judgements, respond to something even more immediate than their own external environment; they act out of a consciousness of Self, they can initiate a Self-Determining force that orders the fruits of complex experience according to inner principles and directives.

It is worth noting that, at this level of being, the gesture of the determining force within human beings shares a strong resonance with that of the stars. However, while the star forces manifest themselves in the most physical linear forms of minerals, they become the forces of Self-Determination manifested in the immaterial realm of Concept and Principle. Both realms reveal an aspect of form that stands the test of time; yet only after this has been raised upwards, through the successive kingdoms, do we see it come to full and free expression in ourselves. The cool light of distant stars has metamorphosed into clarity of thinking.

One can now see that each successive determining force raises creation to a higher plane of being, enabling greater freedom and vitality over increasingly shorter life cycles. We can picture the mineral world as most lacking in freedom, where the life cycle, such as it is, is measured in millions of years. This kingdom is imprisoned in the earth and yet reveals linear forms and structures that appear to sparkle with remembered starlight.

The spiral, vortex forms of the more liquid plant kingdom accompany the life processes of growth and decay, and the life cycle can extend to thousands of years. This kingdom has broken free from, but remains anchored to, the earth, while orientating to the heavens. The animal kingdom has a life cycle typically less than a century except for creatures such as the clam or tortoise that can extend to hundreds of years. However, while animals are free to roam the earth, they are still 'tethered' to their instincts. The human kingdom has the greatest degree of freedom, with a life cycle measured in decades. Human activity is not so strongly restricted by instinct, after basic needs have been met, but is released to be determined instead by freely chosen values and principles that make up our moral conscience. One might say that it is our desire to self-determine our own activity in this way that gives meaning and purpose to our lives. Amongst these purposes can be the study of plants! Plants reveal to us the principle of Life in such a way that we can learn to transform and redeem it.

11

APPLYING THE METHOD TO ROCKS

Wherever we live, however rich the soil may be, one does not need to go very deep to find rock. One may in fact not need to dig at all: rock crops out at the surface. Or at the beach there may be one kind of rock towering above us and a different kind upon which to sit. Where there are cliffs, whether on the beach or inland, perhaps at a road or rail cutting where rock is laid bare, it may be clear that this rock has been laid down over the ages. Sometimes we see layers, strata, which geologists have used, by comparing place with place, to date the epochs when these deposits have been made. Much of this work was begun in the Avon Gorge in Bristol, where many geological epochs are to be seen in the one place (therefore clearly sequencing rocks recognizable from other parts of the country), so high is that cliff face, carved by the river rather than the sea. A modern 'domestic' example is the 'hole in the road', where one can see the different stages of road surface one atop the other. From this it is good to imagine that wherever we walk, these layers are there beneath us. In some places they have been broken through, either by the slow rise of molten rock as 'intrusion' or the dramatic upsurge of a volcano (extrusion). We may recall the white cliffs of Dover or Beachy Head, with their strata of flints that end up making the shingle beaches, or the cliffs of Yorkshire with their inclusions of carnelian or jet. Another kind of cliff may indeed be composed of rock from these intrusions and extrusions, where there may either be no obvious strata or else old layers that have been fused together by Earth's internal heat and then buckled into wave shapes. My favourite example is at Rinsey Head, just west of the Lizard Peninsular in Cornwall, where a vein of granite, a 'granular' composite rock of feldspar, mica and quartz that sometimes gives birth to other minerals, has intruded vertically into the local rock, the whole then being distorted. The result is a dramatic sinuous granite serpent in the cliff with a crown of mauve crystals with its 'dead' image lying flat on the beach. This locality is not far from the Lizard Peninsular with its Serpentine nor from St Michael's Mount. Aeons ago the southern part of The Lizard drifted tectonically from somewhere near Western Africa.

The variety of rock is enormous; and however thoroughly geologists can now describe rocks, an individual rock always provides something new to observe. This chapter attempts to show how a certain approach to rocks may equip the observer with still further experiences. Also with rock one can unlock secrets that are not perceptible to eye or hand and reach into inner processes, as was possible with plants.

Holding a piece of rock, as we did with a leaf, we put out of our mind everything we might already know about it, particularly its identity, and just use our senses. Every perceptible attribute is classed under this method as *form*, the shape of the object being just one aspect of this form. There is the feeling of a certain weight; we might have been struck by an unexpected weight or lightness when we picked it up—if we looked at it before so doing. It has several qualities, found in geological works, that are used for identification. Here we shall just name a few for our purposes: colour, texture, warmth/coolness, odour, tone when struck, and fracture, or the way the rock splits, as flint splits in flakes that are called conchoidal, or shell like and slate splits so evenly flat that it makes good tiles, more so than limestone. These are all aspects of Form. They can be described without much prior knowledge and it is good to spend a while quietly doing this until we can go no further and have described the rock piece to ourselves as best we can. The form has impressed itself upon us through our various sense organs. It is fruitful to do this now with a second sample as was done initially with leaves. This strengthens, through the contrast, the sense of *impression* that is so fundamental to our method, taking it out of the cerebral into the vital, as it is totally objective—our impression is a *fact*; others may have different ones but the fact that we have had a particular impression is totally objective and incontrovertible. Here we reach a frontier between subjective and objective. Our *subjective* impression becomes *objective* when we become conscious of it, for then it has the same validity as anything in the *sense* world (someone can perceive us having it), the reality of which can be held as an open question until we have taken the experience further, just as is sometimes necessary with a sense perception that may have at first deceived.

With leaves it was possible to extract from the varied possible perceptions a basic set of features common to all leaves that characterized 'leaf'. Now the task is to do the same for rocks. The result is not dissimilar—outer surface possibilities, inner structural possibilities—only no stalk and no main stem.

The next step now is to work with a series of samples collected around one attribute, for example sharp edges or similar colour and put them into order. The effort of making a meaningful order deepens our alertness to the objects before us. We have to *supply* the meaning here whereas the plant gave it to us as a development *on one stem*, an important point in the distinction of mineral and plant.

It was an eye-opener for a group of young people travelling towards Tintagel, stopping on the way to practice observation—the 'Merlin exercises'—a phrase coined by the Youth Group I was guiding to Tintagel—to see the colour of the flints in the fields being red in one location and next day blue in another! This observing of contrast works strongly when care has been taken to register the *impression* that we receive of the stone. In this way we open part of ourselves to the experience that our *impression* must be the *expression* of something unseen. We sensed the forces working in the plant as artistic, sculptural ones as they express themselves in the sense world. Here, we move beyond the realm of the human kingdom, so may not anthropomorphise whatever is there. However, we do become able to bring some content to the otherwise abstract statement that 'behind' outer Form is the work of 'Spirits of Form'. By bringing an artistic quality into our thoughts and observations we can reach through to what is hidden for the senses. We do this constantly in many areas of life but usually take this for granted without ascribing anything special to it, unaware that we are on the first step of the path to perceptions of a world beyond. The next stretch of the way is to feel that we are not just following shadow play but the actions of real beings. These observations have the power to transform a piece of theology or mysticism into science that can be verified by anyone willing to do the work of observing totally and giving themselves time to register the deeper effect this has on the observer. To the considerations already made of elementary spiritual beings we now add those of the much greater ones that organise and sustain the universe.

A refinement of this is to take rocks that appear to be the same sort, as far as we can surmise. Suppose, for example, we take several pieces of sandstone. On the whole they are likely to be an orange-yellow but there may be some of very different colours (mauve, brown, green ...) and some with lines of different colour within them. We make a sequence of these. If you live somewhere with no sandstone you can take your local rock, perhaps one of the various types of limestone, or perhaps granite, gneiss or basalt if you live in older geological regions. Before bringing them into order this is like the first random collection of leaves but through ordering them we find that there is an equivalent to 'leaves on a stem': specimens where something of a time sequence is apparent. This might be the degree of smoothing. It might be the increase or decrease in a particular inclusion or of crystal size. We become aware that each rock has its own genesis. Each individual rock is part of a 'becoming'. Suddenly we glimpse that all rocks are part of the one great organism of Earth in *becoming*.

The series we have made will help us unlock this becoming in *one of the single* pieces, which we can now take to examine. We begin to ask questions of the piece before us. For every sense-perceptible feature there is the question, 'How did it come to be like that?' A pebble on the beach is rounded because of the grinding action of other pebbles; but what made the flint and how did it come to be there? How did it get into the chalk of the cliff? Then there is the other side of the question: how might it have still changed further in the future?

Suppose the sample has layers in it. This suggests a periodic deposition of material—from where? Ground down somewhere far away and spread out gradually? Yet now it is 'rock hard'—how has that happened? Was heat involved (are there signs of fusion?) or pressure (are the layers distorted?). Some of the unevenness of such layers is explained by deposition from a river with variable speed and volume of flow. The near future is likely to be only further eroding; but might heat return again to act once more in the farther future?

Goethe carried out research such as this on several field trips, notably on the Brocken, the highest peak of the Harz Mountains in northern Germany, inferring its geological past by pure observation. His method was to go from the static arrangements of rock around him into the processes that caused them to be there *and only there*, to penetrate the greater processes that form our world. Steiner has followed this path in his own way, to see the Earth's surface as the result of the activities of the Spirits of Form and Movement mentioned in Chapters 4 and 5 (see *The Mission of Folk Souls*, GA/CE 121, Lecture 5). Our fantasy may imagine the formation of The Lizard Peninsular as a work of this nature, to reproduce the image of Michael and the Dragon in that part of Britain traditionally regarded as the visiting area of Joseph of Arimathea (tin trader) and his nephew Jesus. Well, the rock on the beach is remarkable whatever other views one may have.

Certain feelings arise with these ponderings. The rock before us dissolves away and great vistas of possibility arise in its place. As experience and knowledge increase, these possibilities narrow down to a fairly clear idea of the processes that led to this rock being just here and in the state in which it was found. A position has been reached comparable to beholding a metamorphosis of a plant, as one phenomenon or entity: something actually *invisible* to the senses yet responsible for the sense object. We have once more reached the work realm of the Spirits of Movement and are helped to grasp geological *time* as an evolutionary *process* instead of a measure of years. The relationship between these two is difficult to quantify just as are those times that run quickly or slowly according to our soul's preoccupation. Gradually, confidence is gained that the soul can be trained to be a very exact observer and on occasion intuitively know better than received knowledge. It is then a test to formulate our convictions so that they are accessible to the understanding of others and perhaps their experience as well. That is the way to confirm that we are on the right track. That is one way of being scientific.

With plants, we would now be comparing metamorphoses to awaken powers of observation and exact imagination to the higher level of Gesture. Here, we can compare the impressions gained from the different series of rocks that we made and sense a movement from line to area—all rocks become felt to be in a mutual interrelationship akin to constant movement. It becomes clearer what 'rock' means: an entity, a being, upon which we stand. It is only a small step from here to wonder whether this being that now lies dead beneath us was ever alive. For many rocks it is known that they do originate in plant or animal material (coal or chalk for example). To perceive *that* in our method would be akin to perceiving, 'beyond' the blossom, the activity of the Being that sends that blossom down out of the 'soul' world into the plant's world of life.

How can we draw nearer to this? What *is* the substance of 'ground' and what is its being? If metamorphosis and gesture are invisible to the senses yet clearly visible to our trained mind, in what world do they have their being? Are we able now to imagine the *being* of the plant and its connections with planetary movements? We made some preparation for this in Chapter 10 and will develop it further in Chapter 15. In the same kind of pictorial thinking that we learn by observing a variety of metamorphoses, it can be imagined that the Spirits of Movement, which we postulated as working 'behind' these, are also active in the planets. Plants are ruled by planets! Their soul 'lives' there; and their uprightness, that depicts their inner entity or being, relates back to the line linking the sun with the centre of the earth. Their being is ever directed to the sun-*sphere*, wherever the sun-body actually is; sun-body meaning not the corpus 93 million miles away 'up there' but the sphere around the earth upon whose surface the visible sun moves. Only one more step brings us to think that for minerals the spirituality is one stage further removed. It is clear that they are a stage less awake than plants and two stages less than animals, so even *less* of their total makeup is manifest in the sense world. Their *being* is truly of the stars beyond the solar system, something that can be illustrated using certain methods of geometry but too complex for the present work.

Each kingdom of Nature builds upon the one below, annulling its outer attributes, replacing them with something further advanced then adding a new main element. We saw that the plant in its *form* overcomes the forms of the minerals of which it is composed. It no longer has a simple geometrical shape but replaces that with an image of its 'life', its stem, leaves and flowers and how they flow together in the life or etheric body. It is actually a *supersensible* entity, filled out with matter that then makes it visible and then behaves like mineral once more when it dies. We noted that the animal, in turn, displaces the plant's life-form with a soul-form, an expression of its soul life, revealed as it moves; but each animal can only move in the way its body prescribes, unlike the human being who can transcend this. See Chapter 10 again then compare the image in Psalm 8 about Man being created a little lower than the angels and with the rest of creation beneath his feet. There is a glimpse into the nature of 'ground' for which we can be grateful: Man supported in his existence by the other kingdoms of Nature, of which he is part, but so that he can go on to develop a potential that transcends Nature.

Going back now to the mineral: its composition is made up of chemical substances, the heart of its long history of formation, transposition, metamorphosis (in the geological sense) and erosion. This composition is what makes the rock respond in its own way to the outer processes that inflict themselves upon it. Different rocks react differently to water, for instance, some dissolving and others not, because of their composition not only of other rocks within but of the chemical elements of which they consist. I have a piece of rock with milky white crystals on it. These are formed clearly at one end but completely decayed into rust at the other. In another sample, a mineral had overlaid a specimen of clearly formed crystals, which had then dissolved away, leaving behind their impress in the first. These are clear examples of the time processes but go into a third area of investigation that takes an important step beyond it. The leading question here becomes, 'What elements and compounds are active in this piece of matter and how do they relate to one another?' Chalk and limestone are both made of calcium carbonate. The calcium is *happily* united with the carbonate. In dolomite, a closely related compound, it is magnesium that is happily united with the carbonate. But not all metals readily make a carbonate! There are inclinations and disinclinations in this magic world of relationships and there are also substances called catalysts that mediate and help elements to combine that would not otherwise do so. We can liken these affinities to souls that group together into kinds of communities, often with their catalysts. This is beyond *time*, where the biography of the rock lodged; it is the 'animal' or soul level of the mineral, with its sympathies and antipathies and fruitful relationships.

The investigation of ancient rocks by measuring radioactive qualities has shown that certain crystals contain two separate kinds of chemical molecule in measurable proportions. The mother crystal is 'liked' by the one and 'disliked' by the other. Measuring these proportions reveals the time elapsed since they were all molten, because the antipathetic one gradually leaves. This technique, rather crudely described and over-simplified here, results in an age being put on these rocks that approaches that calculated for the Earth, Moon and even of the Solar System.

What can such a statement mean?

We here try to imagine the rock to a fourth stage. We go beyond sense observation (space, mineral, *earth*), beyond the imagination of the rock's genesis (time, plant, *water*), beyond the analysis of relationships within its substance (soul, animal, *air*), to the time, or state, before these relationships of substance became settled, to a threshold of evolution beyond which there was no rock: all was flux; and in this liquid and aery flux wove the entities of the different elements as beings of Fire (spirit, Man). We have gone from relationships within the realm of substance to the *beings* of these substances themselves. We have gone from soul to individuality or spirit. One might say, well, there is no research that goes into that era because everything was molten or even gaseous and cannot be measured until it is at least gaseous. This challenges us to think of a state of substance beyond gas—just 'heat'. Science probes that—with the concept of *plasma*—and has reached into concepts of Quantum Physics that scare off ordinary mortals but amongst which is the mathematics that one cannot know where a 'particle' is and at the same time how fast it is going; one has to choose. One has crossed the frontier of the 'ordinary' world both in substance and thought and come to a primal world that reveals itself to be higher and more 'real'. Zen has reached into particle physics with the thought of a particle being in two places at the same time.

There are thus two distinct ways of dating the Earth that both reach the same threshold: its gaseous, then plasmic state or state of pure heat (Fire). The one is through measurements based on the concept of Matter as atomic. This research is scientifically sound and rigorously applied. It stands up to all the objections that have so far been put to it. The other way is as described here, from sense qualities through processes to affinities and then relationships between *beings*. The science that reaches plasma cannot say anything about this for it cannot reach it. The one is a science that has to exclude human feelings; the other *bases itself upon them*, yet only when such feelings transcend their *personal* nature and become objective. People generally doubt that this is possible but the fact that one is wary of self-deception means that one can become ever freer from it. One can also check results with other people. These sciences are now beginning to meet each other, for part of plasma science has reached the experience that the observer does indeed influence the object in the act of observing, something that makes a link to the theme of redemption developed in a later chapter. If, when science reaches the point of wanting to make a hypothesis out of the facts it has observed, it would instead choose to form a question or seek further phenomena, it would remain within the real created world. It would not stray into another, generated by things imagined. Rather would this course *develop* the imagination, i.e. picture-building capacity, into one that finds the *world of beings* that reveal this created world, rather than a 'subatomic' region that eludes relationships of any kind. One may try to distinguish between correctness and reality in these things.

This approach would acknowledge the 4.6 billion years reckoned by radioactive research as the age of the Solar System *as true for the material world*: matter measures matter. However, it would also be able to approach a process with the measure of those creator spirits, Exusiae, Dynamis and Kyriotetes, examined in the last few chapters through Form, Metamorphosis and Gesture and whose outer expression is seen in the movements of this same Solar System. For a long time I puzzled over the fact that Rudolf Steiner seemed to dispute the modern dating of geological epochs, rather expressing time in tens of thousands of years, although in earlier works he did speak of the billions of years as though he accepted them. I had met these discrepancies in other places too but always later realised it was not error but a question of finding the right viewpoint for one's judgement. In this case I owe progress to the work of Jochen Bockemühl, the botanist, and Cornelius Bockemühl, the geologist. ('Erdentwicklung aktuell erfahren' *Geologie und Anthroposophy im Gespräch*, Verlag Freies Geistesleben 1999 Ed. Cornelis Bockemühl.) They brought a meditative mind to bear on it and enabled me to approach the topic in the above manner. *Matter* is measured correctly in billions of years, *spirit* in the rotation of the heavens: the precession of the equinoxes (that disconcerting difference between Zodiacal signs and constellations of actual stars) and the Platonic Year (the time taken to complete one circuit). However, whilst there will always be a logical problem here that can nag away at one's mind and soul for a lifetime, the fourfold approach sketched out here makes it possible to embrace it as a polarity and find an overarching 'impression' of the origin of the earth as a quality of heat, Fire, or Divine Will.

We have penetrated with intuition a state before the earth cooled sufficiently to be visible, in which beings of substance moved freely before they entered into earthly relationships and processes and met us on the beach. Nuclear science halts there because at that point nuclei did not yet exist; our mind, however, does not need to stop there at all. It can tread the path of Anthroposophy with its methods and concepts for those periods. When we have acquired the trust in our own soul responses, supervised by our free spirit, we can 'read' the beings of Nature to the point of meeting them in spirit—that is, in the sense described in this book. We grow thereby and can sense 'knowledge' as a kind of communion, in which we recognise ourselves as the proud pinnacle of Nature and the humble apprentice of the Spirit.

12

APPLYING THE METHOD TO BEES

The queen bee, after hibernation, begins to lay. She places a first egg in the first cell, then continues in adjacent cells, guided by worker bees who encircle her. Although the laid area is roughly circular, Nature varies this and it becomes oval. After three days of laying, during which she also deposits eggs in adjacent frames, the first egg hatches, then the others, so that as she adds ever widening layers of new eggs, there is in the centre a growing ovoid of hatched larvae. The overall volume has *life* awakening at its core, spreading to the outside, where cells previously filled with pollen are cleaned and receive their own new egg. A cross section now shows larvae in the centre surrounded by eggs, surrounded in turn by pollen stores, then nectar and finally capped honey. We see the life-form of an egg in the darkness of the hive.

The method we want to follow is to seek out *forms* then follow the changes they make as they grow or as new forms of the same kind appear later in time. So far, two forms have appeared: the egg and the cross section of a laid area of brood. Biology calls the changes an insect egg goes through *metamorphosis*. We shall look at the metamorphosis of this cross section 'egg' and seek its *gesture*. Later we shall look for the gestures of other aspects of bee life and attempt to read the overall gesture of the bee.

The next stage, eight days after laying and five after the first hatching, is that the larvae become mature enough to be sealed with a fresh wax cap, following which they will mature for a further 13 days before emerging as perfectly formed adults. The section becomes different: where the first egg was laid, there is now an empty cell. Moving outwards is an area of capped cells, then larvae diminishing in size, then eggs. Very soon the first cell will have been cleaned to receive a new egg.

This 21-day rhythm continues, with each band of maturity gradually expanding to the periphery. The oval brood area may continue to grow, becoming greater and more complex; but the 21-day rhythm of bee creation continues throughout the season as a *pulse*. That is the gesture of the brood area: a pulse of life.

The biological metamorphosis from egg to larva to pupa to imago, is a series of *forms*. Progressing throughout the 21-day rhythm from form through metamorphosis to gesture, the gesture of growing bees is captured, at least imaginatively. The pulse of *life* brings forth animal beings, beings of *soul*. The pulse of an animal is a soul gesture.

For the emerged bees there begins another 21-day period of activity in the hive: cleaning, feeding, receiving and storing the harvest being brought in, defence against predators, maturing the nectar into honey, wax-making, cell building and queen feeding and guidance in her laying. These make up the life of the hive performed by beings of soul. After their 21-day period here, they are ready to leave the hive for the last 21 days of their lives (approximately) as foragers. First, however, they must learn how to find the hive entrance again, since their eyesight, though good, is not suited to this. They therefore have to teach their whole *bodies* how to return home. This is done in stages.

If you sit quietly by a hive entrance (after a cautious approach if the first time) and watch the activity there, it first appears totally chaotic but with patience some different types of movement become apparent. Probably the most obvious is that of those bees leaving the hive like little bullets, returning in the same purposeful way. This contrasts with another group that seems purposeless. These bees just fly randomly around the entrance, sometimes nearer, sometimes farther away. After a few visits it becomes apparent that this does not happen throughout the day but usually con-fined to the afternoon. By considering the brood pulse, including the activity of cell construction necessary before eggs can be laid, we see that here the earthly home of a bee colony, their body, is to be discerned. There are *physical* elements, cells and stores, and *life* elements, expressed in the hive activities. Each of these has elements of form, metamorphosis and gesture. The gesture is perceived, as with the other kingdoms of Nature, as something that emerges when *all* the activities and movements are combined and followed in time. Now, with the emergence from the hive, we have two new movements: the foraging, fast flight, and the more 'rambling', though actually no less purposeful, *orientating* flight. A closer look shows that each individual bee, in its wanderings, continuously faces the hive entrance. She is subsequently able to find this without searching for it, as we can find a light switch accurately in the dark. The body knows. The process is then repeated a little farther away; then foraging begins, with a radius of some miles.

There are many other movements to be observed at the hive mouth and still more around the harvesting of nectar, pollen, propolis and water. There are also movements associated with communication, defence, mating and swarming. These are all wonderful to observe. However, to perceive the wisdom in the movement and its purpose for the whole, we need to identify how the form of the *individual* bee moves and how this creates the overall gesture that the *group* makes. Although these are wonderfully described in beekeeping literature, a real knowledge of the bee must surely involve a meeting with the being of the whole hive. Part of the mystery of the plant was to be found in its invisible or spiritual dimension, the 'plant spirit' and its counterpart in thought, the 'idea'. Where are the comparisons of these for the life and nature of bees? In human life we may understand somebody's movements as *movements* but unless we can put these into the context of a human life we have still not met the real person. The interest that we bring to this is the more fruitful the more selfless it is, which means the more honestly appreciative and loving. Observing bees is certainly a wholesome way of learning love and honesty of that kind.

Applying our general method of observation to bees in this way enables us to reach beyond the outwardly apparent to the inner mystery. What may we still discover?

Taken all together, the various *movements* of a bee community reveal the nature of its *soul*, as we found with animals generally. We can say this because observation has shown us that their *body* is revealed in the cell structure, *life* in the first 21-day period and *soul* in the second. Surely no one watching a bee within a flower can doubt this soul element; but it is further revealed when we follow the bees on each forage flight away from the hive. This represents an expansion of the hive being and is true too for the whole day between dawn and dusk. The 'bee' grows from hive-size to the dimension of the locality. Seeing the whole colony as one being like this reveals an analogy with our own waking and sleeping in the rhythm of the day and its variation through the year. This is again a *soul* gesture: expansion and contraction. This hive soul is also something with which one can gradually 'make friends', even converse. An aspect of this is retained in the custom of 'telling the bees', especially about deaths of those connected with them. One comes to the certain feeling that the colony is 'someone'. Beekeepers report receiving messages from their bees, either when something needs attention around the hive or perhaps something quite other. It is a little like someone responsible for a child suddenly having an impulse to check their wellbeing. Why not other enlightenments too?

Observing them using the key 'form—metamorphosis—gesture', bees are seen in the whole perspective of Nature. They have a physical body (comb) within which their life unfolds; and they have a soul life of outer movement in common with other animals.

There is, however, something else within all this movement that is still unaccounted for. This is the swarming activity. This is the time when a rapid exit from the hive does not mean going for forage. It is like a flow. The bees as a whole become fluid!

If one has ever been fortunate enough to see a swarm being hived by shaking it out in front of an empty hive entrance, one will see the decisive moment when all appear to agree to enter and set up home. This becomes a slow steady flow. Moreover, one can tell that there is an overall awareness operating because several will signal the way forward by fanning scent with their wings to those who have not yet found the way. Soon they are aligned to the entrance like iron filings in a magnetic field and flow slowly into the dark interior. It is wonderful to see the queen stepping slowly along with her daughters to begin a new phase of life. Is this significant?

Now, perhaps years later, as the swarm emerges, the orientating movement is reversed but at speed, as though survival depended upon it. If that is marvellous enough, what follows is more so.

A large part of the colony has now swarmed, leaving enough behind to continue living and caring for the brood in the combs. This swarm now makes a stationary cloud near enough to the ground for one to stand in it. Although the cloud as a whole is still, each individual bee is flying to and fro at high speed. This can be frightening unless one has stood within it and realised that no bee ever collides with another, let alone with oneself! They are completely absorbed in their strange activity, clearly a mystery one, inexplicable in three dimensions but easier to understand in a different kind of space. What is happening? All those orientating movements made before the hive mouth at the beginning of their soul life are dissolved away now by this frenetic activity, leaving the 'soul' of that colony finally freed from its earthy home, its body, the place of its life hitherto. Now it is ready to move to a new location in which to lay down a new body.

Our observations recognise this state as an *animal* state but now one in *death* rather than in life. The soul has left the body but it is not dead! Just as the butterfly depicts for us the immortality of the soul, the bee manifests a condition where this soul is able to *establish a new life*.

Will the beekeeper have the delight of seeing this cloud enter another of their own hives or a different kind of altruistic pleasure seeing it fly off to bless another locality? Either way, that swarm will very soon begin to lay down white wax to be chiselled into the well-known piece of skilled craftsmanship that is the comb of hexagonal cells.

A first egg will again be laid. The *movement* of swarming reveals another *gesture*. The soul builds itself *another* body, without parents, then incarnates into it!

Our observations invite us here to recall ideas of repeated human Earth lives but considered now on a level not possible in Earth evolution, where earthly parents are still necessary for man and beast. Are we contemplating the Bee as depicting for us a state of the fourth, human kingdom, as it may come to be in a far future?

13

APPLYING THE METHOD TO COLOUR

Sight opens up for us a world of *colour*. Elements of shape and outline are seen as the interplay of sight, first with the beginning of mental activity that notices the *differences* in the colours then with the sense of *movement* that follows these differences and thereby perceives shape. The word *shape* is used here rather than 'form' since we use 'form' to refer to *any* element of sense perception: individual colours, sounds, smells, textures and so on. These have been referred to as the work of *Spirits* of Form into the sense world. We have worked consistently from forms (leaves) to metamorphoses, the movement that links together a series of leaves from one plant. Then we have gone further, to gesture, the realm of the Spirits of Wisdom where the archetypes of plants reside.

This book describes the way of observing forms so as to behold metamorphosis and to observe metamorphoses so as to grasp gesture. From there it is but a step to a sense for the Being. This can be applied in other parts of Nature too; and here we shall look at colour in this light. However, this is not a work about Art or Colour Theory so the approach will be general, an indication for using a methodical approach to colour observation that leads to a sense for the being of colours and colour altogether.

When an array of all possible colours is observed it is seen that some are just shades of grey, between pure white and pitch black. These greys can be ordered in a line linking these two extremes. Many of the other colours are seen to be tints of these shades of grey. Each shade of grey can move towards a colour hue that ultimately contains no grey at all; similarly with pure white and pure black.

So: one family of 'colours' is 'uncoloured', just black, white or grey. From each colour of this family other families are generated as it moves towards 'coloured colours', until finally no trace of grey is left. These are 'pure' colours.

Yet other families arise when colours are mixed. Mixing two pure colours results either in another pure but 'mixed' colour or in 'broken' colours that begin to have a trace of brown in them. An extension of this family contains admixtures of members of the greys as well.

Thus, upon investigating even the *pure* colours, some are found to be mixtures of others. Well known are green, orange and violet but there are other mixtures that are still pure colours like turquoise, mauve and gold-yellow. In the end all the pure colours arrange themselves in a circle, where each one is, in hue, harmoniously settled between its neighbours. There is no argument possible as to where each colour should go. The movement around the circle is smooth, yet very varied in mood. Moving from orange into red then towards mauve is very different from moving from blue to green to yellow. Colours reveal themselves together as a kind of being. The circle has its own internal character. It is a different kind of entity from the line of greys between black and white.

Our method would then have us arrange members of any of the above colour families into a sequence born out of their own nature, as are the leaves on a stem. Each colour is a 'form', which we observe thoroughly as in 'A Leaf Exercise'. Their sequences could then be called metamorphoses.

One might well feel initially that the sequence of greys from white to black is somewhat uninteresting; but to use the observation method, slowly and thoroughly going along step by step, is an amazing experience, especially when reversing the direction too. One discovers the *gesture* of grey and both its relationship to and contrast with its special cases, white and black.

Doing the same with sequences of the other families begins to articulate the manifold natures within the world of colour. A very special aspect of *form*, *metamorphosis* and *gesture* is gained from the pure colours in relationship to the greys, the uncoloured colours. It was noted above that for each shade of the grey scale one can move towards a colour that no longer bears any trace of grey within it (these metamorphoses all have

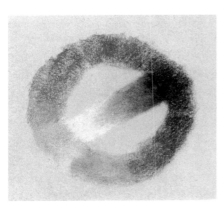

their own strong gestures!). This is a good way of surviving a heavy grey sky: to what colours are the different areas directed? Some of them have already begun their journey and reveal weather patterns or the season.

Now, to compare the colours of the pure circle with the grey scale reveals that the latter can be placed within the circle as a diameter with white near lemon-yellow and black near violet. Apart from these two, all the colours have a partner sharing the same 'value' of brightness or dimness with one of the greys. This reveals another property of the pure colours: they each have, although *pure*, a relationship to 'grey', or more accurately the awkward expressions 'bright–dim' or brightness/dimness, or light/shade. A grey background helps the purity of the colour.

We can think of a mono*chrome* (the word accepts that grey is a colour) picture of a coloured scene. There is a realm of colour distinct from that of light and darkness. The gesture of the coloured picture is different, perhaps more awake, fuller, than the grey one, yet, as the lasting appreciation for monochrome photography indicates, the latter has its own awakeness too. However, thinking of evolution, we can imagine an early world before water existed where only light and matter prevailed, the consequence being the grey scale and its special poles of pure light and pure darkness. This is a 'colour' theory to be found in a number of ancient myths and legends. How different when evolution moves on and there is water—and rainbows. Out of the greys, or rather the black/white polarity, arises our living world; but the study of the gestures of the grey family over against the pure colour family reveals that colour comes 'down' upon the grey world in the same way as the blossom with its colour comes down upon the plant. Everyone knows, of course, that the blossom comes out of the bud on the earthly stem but from the aspect of metamorphosis and gesture it comes out of the soul world to bless and enhance the world of the living. In plants the body of the plant and all its stages of development as described by botany is not the *cause* of the blossom but the *condition for its appearance*. Likewise, the scale of grey and the interplay between darkness and light are not the cause of colour but the condition for its appearance. Is the rainbow in all its majesty and glory adequately explained by a juxtaposition of rain and sun and certain formulae? That's surely a grey idea. Yet they have to be there for us to see the glory.

We step gradually into a different world once we start to unlock the gestures of Nature's processes. Still looking at the sky, just notice that there is air—possibly moist, possibly dusty—and that this affects the quality of the sky's blue and the sun's yellow. Without the atmosphere the sun is white and the sky black (midday sun and midnight sky being an earthly hint of this). Now observe the sequences. The sun from sunrise to sunset goes from a rare red through orange and yellow to white, then back through to red. The sky goes from a deep cobalt blue through to azure and cyan, although white near the sun. Some see it as really violet where the atmosphere is thin.

These colours of sun and sky are seen also on the coloured edges visible through a prism or obliquely through water. There has to be a relationship between dark and light and there has to be a medium of a certain density through which to look, conditions that bring light and darkness into a *dynamic* relationship rather than just mixing passively to grey. It is as though the rainbow is split along its length and separated into two sequences of colour: yellow, orange and red on one side, cyan, blue and violet on the other.

A lovely Australian Aboriginal tale relates that after a day of quelling troubles amongst mortals, the divine Rainbow Serpent, who is painted with red and yellow stripes down his body, takes an evening stroll with his wife, who wears a *blue dress*. We mortals then see the rainbow! The *archetype* of colour is the *two* sequences that appear in their pairs; their relationship is the symbol of harmony between heaven and earth. If the Rainbow divinity and his Spouse have visited us and elevated our minds first, we see in the rainbow the threshold to the world we are trying to visit through the exercises. The Rainbow Serpent is a creator being, working in the place between darkness and light. It is not that light magically contains the rainbow colours locked up inside it but that light and darkness are both needed before they can charm the colours off each other.

We note that yellow and violet are complementary colours as are orange and blue, and red and cyan almost. Returning to a circle of six pure colours we now note that these two pairs make the two sides of the circle. They meet in green below and magenta above. On their own the Serpent and his Wife stop short with red and cyan. They do not reach the magenta above and the green below that would make the third pair of complementary colours until they join together. In several experiments in spectroscopy (where prisms are used), conditions determine part of the outcome by making sure that blue and yellow *do* mix to green. This is then a *secondary* phenomenon, not a primary one and this needs to be taken into consideration when extracting laws from it, especially as the question is begged as to how things would stand were the green to be left unmanifest and the magenta caused to appear. Something upon which to ponder and a challenge to the science of the spectroscope! Some of our modern astrophysics is based on this taking a secondary phenomenon as a primary one.

There are many ways to demonstrate these phenomena. What is

important here is to take yellow and cyan–blue as 'forms' and follow their *metamorphosis* to orange and blue respectively then to red and violet. Just as in leaves there is a jump from the top leaf to the blossom so is there a jump from red and violet to magenta. Whereas the colours in each sequence have been getting gradually darker, in the space where they would meet appears a lighter colour, magenta, a colour from beyond; and whereas in the opposite direction, towards the ground, so to speak, the colours are becoming lighter, their meeting is a mixture—the opposite of a jump—in green, *darker* than either, the picture colour of the living nature of the Earth.

Colour 'appears' within the right, dynamic relationships between light and darkness. It appears through the activity of Form and Metamorphosis within Light and Darkness. The two colour processes come together on the earth for green; but with magenta the *Gesture* appears from above of that realm of the Spirits of Form, Motion and Wisdom. They endow a Being from their ranks with this colour to allow us 'down here' a vision of that realm.

> Sun—Yellow ... Orange and Red.
> Sky—Blue (Cyan) ... Indigo and Violet;
> Mixture Green ... enhancement Magenta.

Illustration: gaze at the image below for half a minute then fix your gaze at the space on the right. The after-image appears—as itself but inverted! With care, the colours will be exactly the same—but more shining! The

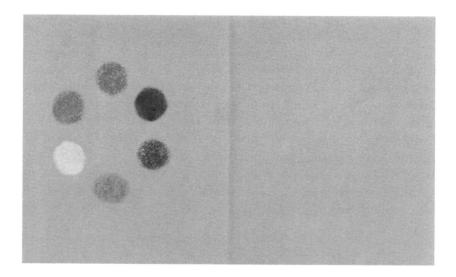

grey background will minimize the colour bias of the after-image that occurs when plain white is used. The new background would also be darker, as well as the new colours.

Complementary colours: Yellow—Violet Blue; Cyan—Orange Red; Magenta—Green.

Form: Yellow;   *Metamorphosis*: Yellow—Orange—Red;   *Gesture*: Magenta (left hand side)
Form: Blue;   *Metamorphosis*: Cyan—Blue—Violet;   *Gesture*: Magenta (right hand side)

14

REDEMPTION OF THE BEINGS OF NATURE AND OF THE EARTH: JOINING UP A DIVIDED WORLD

In 'Looking at Flowers', the feeling arose of an 'elementary being' connected to every plant. It can also be called an *elemental* being in so far as it relates to the elements: earth, air, fire and water. This plant spirit, however, also embraces the activities of the primary beings of the elements in the relationships of the plant to the earth through Earth, Water, Air and Fire. It has connections to each of them. The moist earth where the seeds germinate and the roots grow and draw in nutrients is the domain of the elemental beings of the earth, or gnomes. The region of moist air where the leaves unfold in growth and the plant chemistry of photosynthesis is the domain of water beings or undines, nymphs. That of warm air is the place of sylphs or air sprites who serve the blossoms and the birds in their journeyings along the warmth-paths in the air. Lastly, the concentrations of fire and light within the blossom, the place of pollination, fructification and ripening, give a home to fire spirits or fire sprites or, in older language, salamanders. They are closely connected to pollinating insects, especially in their movements of bliss as they hum within the flower, which they have found through following these fire spirits, rather as undines lead frogs from far away to discover a newly constructed pond.

In one sense the plant spirit is slightly higher than these elemental beings yet in another it is of a more fleeting existence. All these beings are *elementary* in the sense that they have no eternal being, as Man does, or as do the archetypal spirits of plants and animals. They are under *metamorphosis,* and change their role from one condition to another. One may feel that some gnomes have a very long 'life', going back to the beginning of Earth evolution, even earlier. Water spirits on the other hand have very little permanence as they are in constant flux, the essence of watery nature, although the water spirit of a river has more duration than those of its various waterfalls and would last as long as that river existed. There was probably some kind of water spirit born as atmospheric vapour became liquid in primeval epochs. Shakespeare describes through the mouth of Oberon, in *A Midsummer Night's Dream*, the journey around the world of the King of Elementals to visit all the great rivers as part of his responsibility as king of the fairies. This envisages a spirit of a higher rank and duration than those of the individual rivers themselves.

One can gradually sense that within these elemental realms there are hierarchies of being. It was clear to an eastern consciousness that when a tree reaches a certain degree of maturity it acquires its own deva. These 'superior' ones have more 'duration'. The same applies to the beings of the upper elements of air and fire. In general they are even more fleeting than water spirits yet fire spirits acquire duration where a herdsman makes a real soul connection to his animals and dog or beekeepers to their sons and daughters.

We also suggested that the plant spirit needs something from the human being who looks upon it. We noted the poet's phrase 'the look of flowers that are looked at' as a sign of the possibility of there being such a being. How can we develop a wider view here?

Our plant spirit has, we have felt, an expectation, a hope, that we, the beholder, will bless it. A blessing is something given to one who lacks, by one who has; and the plant lacks the indwelling soul and spirit that we possess. These but touch the plant as it were from outside, in the blossom. We have discovered, however, through exercises such as those outlined here, a touch of the soul nature and the archetypal spirit nature of our plant, at the same time becoming aware that we indeed also have a soul and spirit nature within us. This is a bond between Man and Plant (or animal or mineral or the weather and the motions of the heavens): the human soul may choose freely to enter into the process of blessing or remain in the disposition of enjoyment and utility. This blessing is not necessarily a cosmic *duty* for it is only beneficent when bestowed in freedom and love. The beauty that the eye of the beholder generates for the plant is one filled with *knowledge* too and thus embraces the plant being. Let us call it a *cosmic potential*, an opportunity to create. However, in a lecture in Vienna (GA 223 'Michaelmas Soul', Lecture 2, 28 September, 1923) Steiner describes the turning point for the plant once it has been 'seen'. When blessed, that being undergoes a metamorphosis, remaining 'elementary' yet transposing to a higher order of cosmic activity. Put simply, this means being emancipated from Nature for work in the *human* realm. For example, we need sometimes to fill out an idea with mood and colour for some practical project: these beings help with this. Finding lost references, lost thoughts, lost anything; helping over tricky encounters; all sorts of intimate human involvements: here we may sense their work. In this realm they serve the higher spirits of the departed, which according to Steiner reach down into the aura of the blossoms. They bless us as we once blessed them; yet it would be too abstract to imagine it as somehow the same being in a different category as though a tramp we had once fed reappears in our life as a care worker. When we moved from individual leaf forms to their metamorphosis we had to raise our thinking into an artistic mode. So here too; we are looking at forces, at expressions of will, of beings *above* these elementary ones. These may be souls of the departed or angelic beings who want to help our life be fruitful. Thus the emancipated being acts as a focus for helpful spiritual forces connected with our own life. A superstitious feeling for occurrences in the home, for example, becomes a cognition of real and helpful relationships that facilitate ordered and sometimes prophetic actions on a quite humble level, which may then have quite special results of a higher kind.

But what if the plant is not blessed? It is still taken out of Nature and put into the human realm but now in the opposite way, adversarially. What explains the increase in previously unknown viruses and other sub-natural forces that bring illness? What about crowd hysteria, epidemics of fear, indeed epidemics of antipathy or materialism, or even of Spiritism? Are not these qualities the opposite of those to be seen in those that blessed? Yet all of us suffer these qualities too and to sort them out through our own forces is another cosmic challenge and opportunity.

When the observer went through all the stages of grasping form and metamorphosis and reached a feeling for the plant's gesture, this was like forming an inner seed of that plant, yet one not in matter but 'spirit', inwardly. One may say it was 'only in the mind', hence unreal; but through the methodical work that progressed from the mind to heart and breath, then to the limbs, the organs of gesture, one has gained a different view.

Not only is this objective rather than merely subjective (because based on the outside world rather than our soul inclinations) but has been built up, created, in that part of us that transcends Nature. This is our human 'self' or non-selfish ego and is therefore no longer subject to Nature's laws and the passing away of everything to do with the sense world. We have created in our soul what the plant lacks, its soul-spiritual components. The picture may be further enhanced. When we sleep, our body in bed has then a kind of plant nature while our soul and ego abide in regions beyond the sensory (regions we have also entered consciously in a rudimentary way through the exercises). When we are awake and behold the kingdoms of Nature in the way we are learning to do, it is as though we embrace their soul and spiritual parts in our own soul and spirit. Our loving observing is then like a waking up for Nature: her soul and spirit enter her as does ours in the morning. We give to a part of her the blessing of going beyond the end of Earth evolution to become part of the foundation of a new one, like a seed, a gesture.

In short, as both science and the Gospel describe, Nature will pass away, the earth will one day end 'but my words will not pass away' (Luke: 21, 33). This hints at what is here being attempted. These words are 'logoi', the plural for 'in the beginning was the *word*', that created everything. This is not an attempt to use the Gospel as a kind of magical justification of outlandish ideas but a reference to this higher order of mentality we have explored through the exercises. That is an earthly reality that *throws light on the Gospel* rather than the other way round. When I have grasped intuitively the inner and 'eternal' being of the plant, I connect in my consciousness its ephemeral nature to something eternal: 'thoughts' become 'words that will not pass away'.

If anyone carries some kind of picture of Christ as Logos, the divine word and macrocosmic counterpart of the unique human being, Jesus, one may regard Him as the author of this new creation. His creativity is, beginning now in our time, *in partnership* with human beings rather than a unilateral divine act. The kind of work here described belongs to this, for both the elemental beings and the hierarchical beings discovered along the way belong to this macrocosm, to his wider being. They are the members of his macrocosmic self. To attain his goal as Redeemer, he creates by uniting himself and his power with our efforts to transform what lived in Nature. As we bring to birth within our own soul Nature's *higher* elements, the ones not manifest on earth, that we discover, i.e. *uncover*, through this work, we make ourselves into a part of this new kind of creative process. The life of Nature on earth does not immediately *look* different as a result but a spiritual sight would behold the substance of eternity within the temporal. We develop further Eliot's rose vision to the level of sensing the plant spirit and the redemption of the natural order through the greater Spirit.

There is beauty and goodness in the cosmic order. This means that even those beings now compelled to wreak havoc and create suffering in human lives may also be redeemed. It is comparable to a child who does not flourish in class but constantly tries to please the teacher in its own way. If these attempts are rejected, the child may inwardly rebel and become actively disruptive and destructive, hating what they wanted to be able to love. The cosmos is generous in the opportunities it offers to human beings and we may apply the same approach to this order of creation that was applied to plants: observing their appearances and metamorphoses and sensing their gestures. Then we can look at the spirituality behind everything and try to intuit its ways. We then work with loving appreciation and empathy for these beings that we and humanity have pushed to where they now are. That is a concomitant of human free will: the world tolerates our learning-mistakes to give us time and opportunity to redeem them. We can bring recognition to fear, stability to hysteria, materialism and so on. In this way we rob the adversarial forces of their nourishment and starve them out. By then we have also learned to receive and utilise the good things that these one-time adversaries also bestow, like freedom and intelligence.

At the same time thereby the ranks of beings able to help humanity progress in freedom and goodness are swelled.

Given the right care, our sensitivity to others too may be enhanced. By comparison with the foregoing, would not the outlook for the world become more golden?

15

AN ASTRONOMICAL CONCLUSION

Through the foregoing we saw that the line joining the centre of the earth to the sun is imaged in the upright stem of the plant, and that the planets going round the earth were imaged in the leaves spiralling around it. The 'spirit' of the plant, its *being*, is gestured in the stem that connects the life of the earth to the sun, whilst its soul is gestured in the way these leafy spirals culminate in the blossom, bringing the spiral back to the centre again. The separation that began with germination is reunited. In this image, the plant reveals something more than a piece of botany.

From early childhood I wondered at the stars and knew they had a message. Later, as a young teenager, I was being escorted home one night by a friend's father. 'Look,' he said, 'that's Mars and that's Venus.' It is certainly possible that impolitely I did not respond verbally to this kind piece of information that most people would not have been able to impart; but I was thinking, 'How do you know that?' and anyway, 'What difference does it make to my life?' All remained a riddle. I found no access to those mysteries, not even in my school's Astronomy Club and by then my friend had moved away. Years later I beheld a triangle of bright stars in the western twilight. I had a sense some must be planets for they had not been there a fortnight earlier; and they were telling me something I could not at the time understand. The gesture of this triangle was so strong, although it weakened during the following evenings before going silent. Not long afterwards, however, someone did reveal a way towards understanding that message. The soul certainly knows much but the mind cannot always interpret it. Although one should keep a scientific scepticism about any interpretation since the whole personality can bias it, the initial pure impression that stars have a message for mankind should at least be treated seriously. These impressions bypass the source of error within us: let them remain on a back shelf in the soul until their time of revelation comes. Ancient traditions and some recorded instances of this are plentiful. Again, Psalm 8 speaks of the starry sky as the 'work of Thy hands'. One more step and we sense, they *are* the hands. The psalmist was addressing Jahwe, one of the creator Spirits of Form (Elohim), who bring the heavens into sense perception out of their inner mobility of divine thought. Above spirits of this rank, others whose working has been discussed, are the Spirits of Movement and Wisdom or Dynamis and Kyriotetes. It is therefore not too far-fetched to regard the stars really as the fingers of a higher creativity. This creativity writes messages in the sky that invite interest and research into matters of the heavens.

It was Karl Mier, whom I have already mentioned, who opened this up for me in the 1960s and to whom I owe an enormous debt of gratitude.

Our approach would bring another exercise to his: to look at a planet as a *form*, follow its path, then from repeated observations of it, read its gesture. I can still see my other great teacher, Frits Julius, in his plant course, sweeping his arm widely in the gesture of Mars, showing how it is replicated in the impulsive curved branches of shrubs that are followed by another powerful curve in the following growth season, with lesser branches dying back, as in the fruitful elder.

Then one would take the constellations as a *picture form* that changes, undergoes *metamorphosis*, in the course of the year. The relationship to be won is so strong that one can have quite a shock when, having travelled a good distance further north or south, one notices the change to the sky. Something in the soul, almost in the subtle layers of the body too, has to adapt. This is extreme when one changes to the southern hemisphere, where the sun goes round the other way ...

In the end, one lives in the feeling that one is in the centre of a universe that speaks its secret language and influences all life secretly with its inherent powers but that these powers are not abstract forces but great beings. This includes the gift of creativity alluded to above, which is the tool of our ego, our humanity, in the work of the care of the Earth, its husbandry, that will serve it and bring out its best. This feeling develops steadily as we tread the hard path of the exercises laid out here, put together as they are from phrases of Rudolf Steiner and the expositions of his pupils. This feeling is one of coming of age in a cosmos that is spiritually populated. It is neither a vacuum nor filled with various kinds of inanimate matter or anti-matter but *beings*, not aliens but belonging to the furtherance of humanity. They are beneficent and give one the evolutionary task of knowing their creation in such a way that it has a future that goes beyond this earth-time. These beings, from the lofty to the elemental, have placed us in this creative potential so that the cosmos will not go on out of the same order but be recreated in a new way by us human beings. Every time we observe the existing world in the ways described, we make a modest contribution to this. Our knowledge becomes the seed that in the earth dies, to develop in a way as yet unforeseen in the future.

In our mind we may now return to the first leaf we examined and remind ourselves that it is not isolated in the cosmos but connected to all. We try to feel this starry system moving around it, together with the great creators of the universe and the faithful spirits of the elements. To these we may add the thought that the growing plant is also surrounded, within the light, by the souls of the departed. Their influence gradually changes the world, eon by eon. We too shall one day join in that activity. We experience our Self standing between these two worlds, an ego that is growing by redeeming the smaller for its place in the future of the greater, yet in such a way that the greater, with its great Beings of Spirit, is totally transformed by having passed through our loving gaze, armed with the question, 'What *can* you see?'

Observing may reveal much of Nature's Secret.

A NOTE FROM RUDOLF STEINER PRESS

We are an independent publisher and registered charity (non-profit organisation) dedicated to making available the work of Rudolf Steiner in English translation. We care a great deal about the content of our books and have hundreds of titles available – as printed books, ebooks and in audio formats.

As a publisher devoted to anthroposophy...

- We continually commission translations of previously unpublished works by Rudolf Steiner and invest in re-translating, editing and improving our editions.

- We are committed to making anthroposophy available to all by publishing introductory books as well as contemporary research.

- Our new print editions and ebooks are carefully checked and proofread for accuracy, and converted into all formats for all platforms.

- Our translations are officially authorised by Rudolf Steiner's estate in Dornach, Switzerland, to whom we pay royalties on sales, thus assisting their critical work.

So, look out for Rudolf Steiner Press as a mark of quality and support us today by buying our books, or contact us should you wish to sponsor specific titles or to support the charity with a gift or legacy.

office@rudolfsteinerpress.com
Join our e-mailing list at www.rudolfsteinerpress.com

RUDOLF STEINER PRESS